Nuclear New Mexico

American Wests

SPONSORED BY WEST TEXAS A&M UNIVERSITY

Bonney MacDonald, General Editor

Nuclear

A HISTORICAL, NATURAL, AND VIRTUAL TOUR

New Mexico

M. Jimmie Killingsworth and Jacqueline S. Palmer

with photographs by James E. Frost

TEXAS A&M UNIVERSITY PRESS College Station

This paper meets the requirements

of ANSI/NISO Z39.48–1992 (Permanence

of Paper).

Binding materials have been chosen

for durability. Manufactured in the

China through FCI Print Group

♾

Library of Congress Cataloging-in-Publication Data

Names: Killingsworth, M. Jimmie, author. | Palmer, Jacqueline S., author. |
   Frost, James E., photographer.
Title: Nuclear New Mexico: a historical, natural, and virtual tour / M.
   Jimmie Killingsworth and Jacqueline S. Palmer; with photographs by James
   E. Frost.
Description: First edition. | College Station: Texas A&M University Press,
   [2018] | Series: American Wests | Includes bibliographical references and
   index. |
Identifiers: LCCN 2018006311 (print) | LCCN 2018012640 (ebook) | ISBN
   9781623496890 (ebook) | ISBN 9781623496883 | ISBN
   9781623496883 (flexbound with flaps: alk. paper)
Subjects: LCSH: New Mexico—Guidebooks. | New Mexico—History, Local. |
   Nuclear weapons—New Mexico—Guidebooks | Nuclear weapons—New
   Mexico—History—20th century. | Landscapes—New Mexico. | Natural
   history—New Mexico. | American literature—New Mexico—History and
   criticism. | New Mexico—In literature. | Atomic bomb in literature. |
   LCGFT: Guidebooks.
Classification: LCC F794.3 (ebook) | LCC F794.3 .K55 2018 (print) | DDC
   978.9—dc23
LC record available at https://lccn.loc.gov/2018006311

We have had the bomb on our minds since 1945.
It was first our weaponry and then our diplomacy,
and now it's our economy. How could we suppose
that something so monstrously powerful would
not, after forty years, compose our identity? The
great golem we have made against our enemies is
our culture, our bomb culture—its logic, its faith,
its vision.—E. L. Doctorow (quoted in Bird and
Sherwin, *American Prometheus*, xii)

Photograph of the first atomic explosion displayed on the fence surrounding Trinity Site

Contents

Foreword, *by Bonney MacDonald* / ix

Preface / xiii

Acknowledgments / xv

Part 1   The Historical Tour WHERE EVERYTHING CHANGED 1

Trinity / 6

Bosque del Apache / 26

Spaceport America / 37

Alamogordo / 38

Carlsbad / 39

Los Alamos / 49

Bandelier National Monument / 65

Albuquerque / 78

Sandia Peak   / 93

Part 2   The Shadow Tour DARK LEGACIES 101

Grants Mineral Belt   / 101

Church Rock   / 115

Four Corners / 122

Dulce / 143

Roswell / 150

Valley of Fires / 156

Part 3   The Literary Tour 161

The Epic Literature of Modern Times; or See You in the Funny Papers / 162

New Mexican Novels and Poems: The Power of Words and Witchery / 169

Parting Thoughts TOUR, QUEST, PILGRIMAGE / 190

Bibliography / 193

Index / 197

Foreword

The West Texas A&M University series within the Texas A&M University Press is titled "American Wests" for reasons very much having to do with this book. M. Jimmie Killingsworth, Jacqueline S. Palmer, and James E. Frost have produced a book about *plural* Wests—in this case the complicated, nostalgic, and disturbing landscapes of the Land of Enchantment, or in the words of current billboards and state pamphlets, "New Mexico True." Exactly what we know to be true and hope to be true about this beautiful land is rendered in engaging and sometimes troubling detail in this enlightening volume. *Nuclear New Mexico* will invite you in (it is, after all, both "more and less than a guidebook"), and it will then ask you to put the land at arm's length so that you might—after taking a deep breath—enjoy and interrogate the sights you encounter. The book offers neither just a finger-wagging exposé on environmental damage nor a chamber-of-commerce celebration of an enchanted region, but it offers a tour through the New Mexico we don't always see from the roadside or learn about through the historic signs and roadside stops—a "shadow tour" of the boom and bust cycles of tourism and mining and a sketch of the environmental fallout and the cultural consequences that have followed those often familiar cycles in America's Wests.

Environmentally, we know about the Trinity Site, we know about the experiments at the Sandia Lab, and we know—from our history books—about the projects developed at Los Alamos. We don't, however, always know the backdrop, or the "shadow" stories, that led up to those experiments. In the case of Oppenheimer, for instance, and the project that would emerge during WWII: Who would know that a man named Harry Goulding, who managed to buy a private piece of land from the state of Utah in Navajo Country in the 1920s to open up a trading post for tourists, would one day sell part of that land to John Ford and launch the landscape of American Western film? And who knew that the same Harry Goulding would one day convince the rightfully suspicious Navajos to help scout for and mine uranium to further the war effort? The logic of Goulding's appeal remains stunning: To convince the skeptical Navajos near Church Rock that the yellow powder should be taken from the ground rather than left there, as their legends had advised, Goulding argued that the yellow uranium ore was the same color as the Navajo's precious corn pollen. Both were good and strong for the Navajo people, and besides, the yellow dirt could help the soldiers. The Navajo bought the argument and accepted the scouting and mining jobs, and they prospered until they didn't. They prospered until the Rio Puerco—their water for drinking, livestock care, and crops—became polluted from a spill that released ninety-three million gallons of radioactive water into the river. The sites, like this one near Church Rock, stand as the "forgotten, neglected, [and] nearly erased locations associated" with mining, testing, and land usage in New Mexico.

That said, this book is less didactic than such an example might suggest. In its tour through the land where "terror and beauty, aggression and idealism" are "intertwined," *Nuclear New Mexico* offers balanced juxtapositions. The sublimities of Carlsbad Caverns receive their just due and are located—in the book as they are in life—right near the Waste Isolation Pilot Plant. Indeed, this kind of contrast represents the high notes that emerge when we truly read these landscapes. As we learn, the language of the Atomic Age and the Cold War on the one hand and the vocabulary of environmentalism and preservation on the other often stand right next to each other. Indeed, the rhetoric of the Cold War comes of age just as the rhetoric of the environmental movement gains momentum. Oppenheimer and Leopold are oddly right next to each other in this portrait of place in New Mexico: "for nearly every roadside stop that tells of nuclear history, there's a corresponding monument to natural preservation."

Culturally, too, Killingsworth, Palmer, and Frost unveil and reword what we know about this era already but perhaps might not have voiced entirely. In our "shadow" knowledge, we know that not only were history and the environment changed by what took place at Los Alamos, at Trinity, at Nagasaki, and Hiroshima, but we also know that our world and our way of thinking was permanently altered. On a level that entertained tourists for decades, of course, WWI and the Cold War created a nostalgia that would color ads for Route 66 motels and would later structure the visual props of *Thelma and Louise*. Indeed, a "nostalgia for the 1950s signals the moment that New Mexico entered the mainstream American imagination." The Cold War "feels nostalgic for boomers [so much so that the] . . . fifties were nostalgic even in the fifties." The Cold War and the insignia we associate with roadside motels, even with the armaments of war, go deep in our imagination of an American golden age.

The cultural consequences go deep as well, as we know. Nuclear power "modifies the human way of understanding the world" and hints at the god-like powers long before trumpeted by Nietzsche. Our "awareness of human power" grew exponentially and the projects at Los Alamos and the tests at Trinity thus constituted not merely a world changing "experiment," but also shaped the *experience* of modern humanity." In addition to creating a realization of human power from which we could not return, nuclear power became packaged for the public in ways that would become further internalized in the American psyche. The power and inconceivable damage, along with a war victory to be celebrated, confused an American public. We needed reassurance and we got it. The placards and signage at New Mexico's nuclear museums and tourist sites seem to suggest that we are "safe"—they "seem oriented to justification." The cultural result is what Freud knew well: we bury our worries but wonder, just the same, about the troubling "relationship of secrecy to power." Little wonder that the "world would not be the same."

Nostalgia can delight and give comfort, and, if examined closely, it can unveil backstories and sites we hadn't seen. This book on the legacy of place in a landscape shaped by winds and rain, by centuries of human and animal habitation, and by nuclear experimentation and modern science can tempt us with nostalgia and awaken us to an accurate legacy of place—it can help us to see New Mexico True.

Bonney MacDonald
Series Editor

Preface

Part travel writing, part nature writing, and part cultural commentary, this book unveils a remarkable landscape and beloved homeplace transformed by the atomic bomb—not so awfully and traumatically as Hiroshima and Nagasaki, of course, but no less permanently and definitely. In this sense, the state of New Mexico appears as a microcosm for every other place on the planet. And yet it is its own place—unique and captivating to travelers of many kinds, including those peculiar creatures of recent times: the ecotourist and the nuclear tourist, among whom we count ourselves, your guides.

By calling the book a tour, we're being partly literal and partly metaphorical. Certainly, you can go to the places we discuss—we're not making them up, as outrageous as they sometimes seem. But the book is both more and less than a guidebook. It doesn't guarantee your safety; it doesn't even guarantee to get you to (or into) the various sites. The sites may not be there by the time you arrive; it's an evolving landscape. Going there is a possibility, but not a requirement. That's where the metaphors take over. Driving and walking become metaphors for reading. When we say "drive on," we mean read on, if you please, and take the virtual tour, if you dare.

The tour begins with the most famous sites, many of them connected with the Manhattan Project, which built the first atomic bomb. The project was headquartered in New Mexico during World War II in the secret mesa-top city of Los Alamos, and the bomb was first exploded in the Trinity test in the wild land between Socorro and Alamogordo. Leaving behind the best-known sites, our tour winds through forgotten, neglected, nearly erased locations associated with uranium mining and with mysterious secrets written into the land by decades of government research, extractive technology, and military testing. This part we call the shadow tour, the counterpart of the historical or official tour. Finally, the tour leaps out of the landscape and into the literature of the Atomic Age, from superhero comics to some of the finest examples of indigenous fiction and poetry that New Mexico has to offer—all part of the heritage of Nuclear New Mexico.

We include side trips to destinations that may at first seem only marginally connected to the nuke tour. We go to natural and archaeological sites because, as we hope to show, ecotourism and nuclear tourism have much in common. We offer a brief subtour of missile-and-rocket facilities in tribute to the close kinship of the Space Age with the Atomic Age. And so on. The side trips provide perspective, show how the influence of atomic culture appears in unexpected places, and suggest how deeply the presence of nuclear power modifies the human way of understanding the world.

As writers and photographers, we make no personal claims to special expertise in matters of history and science related to nuclear energy, but draw on the many good books available and other sources of information, including museums and some interviews (listed in the bibliography). We make no attempt to offer an insider's or expert's perspective, but write from the viewpoint of the general public, sometimes denigrated as mere tourists, curious onlookers, rubberneckers in heavy traffic, but sometimes elevated to the status of modern-day pilgrims, in search of meaning in the surfaces and sights that greet them along the road. Like other ecotourists and nuclear tourists who have come to New Mexico before us, we're drawn to the place, intrigued by its culture, intoxicated by the beauty of the land, and fascinated by the history of the state that calls itself the Land of Enchantment. We hope our virtual tour will draw others to ponder what has become of not just New Mexico, but all the lands we love.

Acknowledgments

A strong community of readers helped us along the way. Myrth Killingsworth, the writer (and daughter of two of your tour guides), offered many fine insights on the text and shared formative conversations during the writing. Special thanks go to Carrie Frost for navigation and location scouting during photographic expeditions. We also benefited from the understanding and expertise of the Honorable Peggy Nelson, our dear friend, fellow musician, and retired northern New Mexico district judge. Peggy introduced us to the Honorable Joe Caldwell, another retired judge interested in restorative justice, who provided a wealth of information in our informal talks. Others who helped us with their special knowledge and skills include Phaedra Greenwood and Chipper Thompson, fellow writers from the Taos community. Chipper, also a visual artist and outstanding musician, drew the map of Nuclear New Mexico included in the book. The New Mexico Humanities Council has included "Nuclear New Mexico: The Tour" in its speakers' bureau for several years, offering us the opportunity to work on our ideas with academic audiences and the general public in New Mexico. Duane Benally and Helena Skow of the *Navajo Times* provided generous access to the archives of the newspaper. Travel and lodging for a pair of South Texas presentations were generously provided by the College of Liberal Arts at the University of Texas Rio Grande Valley. We gratefully acknowledge the good advice and strong encouragement we received from two professional reviewers commissioned by Texas A&M University Press, Professor Robert Johnson and Professor Tarla Rai Peterson. We owe our deepest appreciation to the staff at the press, with strong leadership from director Shannon Davies and expert guidance from our editor Stacy Eisenstark.

Nuclear New Mexico

Nuclear
New Mexico
(by Robert
Chipper
Thompson)

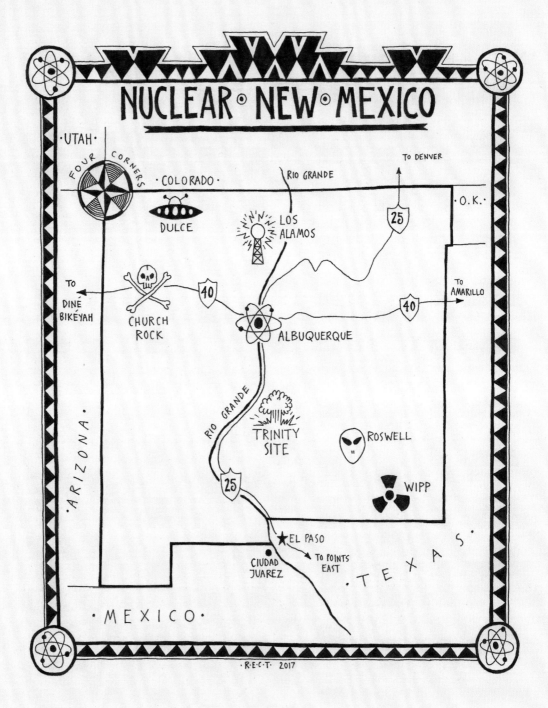

The Historical Tour
Where Everything Changed

First there was ecotourism. Now there's nuclear tourism. The two have more in common than you may think. When the first atomic bomb exploded at Trinity Site and Robert Oppenheimer invoked the famous phrase "destroyer of worlds," the destiny of the environmental movement—"saving the planet"—also sprang into being. The power to destroy and the power to save the earth, once allotted to the gods, fell into human hands for the first time in history. Monstrous threats and great promises competed for attention. A new mythology swept the world, at the center of which stood the Empowered Human of the Atomic Age. The capability to wage global thermonuclear war and place life itself in jeopardy was matched by the claims of environmentalists that human beings have the power, if not the will, to save the planet, to realize the full potential of what environmental dreamer Mark Lynas has called "the God Species."

In the state of New Mexico—where the atomic bomb was first developed and tested—for nearly every roadside stop that tells of nuclear history, there's a corresponding monument to natural preservation: Trinity Site, bordered by the Bosque del Apache National Wildlife Refuge; Los Alamos, sandwiched between the Valles Caldera National Preserve and Bandelier National Monument; and the Waste Isolation Pilot Plant (WIPP) site, weirdly mirrored by Carlsbad Caverns National Park. The landscape bears the imprint of modern humanity, the two-sided image of destroyer and savior of the planet. The image is mapped onto the land just as surely as it shapes contemporary culture, not only world politics and the history of science,

Tourists posing at the Ground Zero monument

but also world literature (indigenous and invasive), popular fiction, movies, and especially comics and graphic novels.

In 2015, Congress authorized the Manhattan Project National Historical Park, with three official sites: Hanford, Washington; Oak Ridge, Tennessee; and Los Alamos, New Mexico. With this act of Congress, nuclear tourism officially arrived, and New Mexico appeared on the map of chosen destinations. But from the start, atomic power was linked with tourism in the state. Robert Oppenheimer, the father of the bomb, spent his vacations near Pecos in northern New Mexico as a sickly and unsociable adolescent, enjoyed the mountains on foot and horseback, discovered his best friends, and made it his place. As the scientific director of the effort to build the bomb, he more or less talked military commander General Leslie Groves into designating remote New Mexico as the secret site of the Manhattan Project. The local population proved malleable or movable, subject to the demands of a mighty government at war. So it was that another layer of secret knowledge was folded into the ancient hills and canyon lands, a modern companion to the age-old myths and rituals that have enlivened this landscape for centuries. Physicists from all over the free world hiked and skied as relief from the work of developing the bomb to stem the fascist tide and allegedly make war impossible. Terror and beauty, aggression and idealism were entwined in the Land of Enchantment. New Mexico became the nuclear navel of the world.

The natural beauty of the state, coupled with the allure of its resources, also assured it a role in the history of environmentalism, which in the postwar years morphed from the old conservationism into a more grandiose and all-encompassing global phenomenon. The state's economy was deeply tied to the extractive industries: first the mining for gold, silver, and lead, followed by the energy rush for coal, oil, and gas, before the powerful pull of uranium came into play. The economy also depended on ecotourism (mainly hiking, camping, and photo touring) and amateur archaeology (scouting the petroglyphed paths and architectural ruins of the state), in addition to the more traditional tourism of sightseeing, hunting, fishing, trail riding, dude ranching, and downhill skiing. Aldo Leopold, the celebrated author of *A Sand County Almanac* and the father of rangeland ecology, had his first assignment in the US Forest Service in New Mexico; he championed the nation's first wilderness area, the Gila, forty years before the passage of the Wilderness Act. Edward Abbey, nature writer and inspiration for activist groups like Earth First!, went to college in Albuquerque, as did the Native American author Leslie Marmon Silko, whose novel *Ceremony* is perhaps the greatest modern fiction to confront the changes brought about by atomic power and modern war on indigenous peoples and their homelands. John Nichols's novel *The Milagro Beanfield War*, with its themes of ecopolitical conflict over rights to water and land among the tricultural elements of northern New Mexico (Hispanic, Indigenous, and Anglo), was made into a feature film by Robert Redford. No course in environmental literature is complete without the New Mexican writers and their stories. Then there are names like Udall and Richardson, familiar to every history of environmental government, on the rolls of New Mexican representation to Washington.

These days, the results of overgrazing, wildlife management, public land policy, water politics, and environmental injustice are intertwined with the legacies of the Atomic Age in New Mexico. It is the place to learn that the environmental movement is permanently and inexorably linked to the advent of the atomic bomb. Sure, the conservation movement has been advocating protection of natural resources and wilderness values since the days of Henry David Thoreau and John Muir in the nineteenth century. But saving-the-earth environmentalism as we know it today really dates from the mid-twentieth century and the onset of nuclear power.

The new atomic human, conceived at Los Alamos and delivered at Trinity Site, realized its destructive identity in Hiroshima and Nagasaki and came of age in the next three decades, during the Atomic Age, whose first iteration brought on the Cold War. The scientists who remained at Los Alamos contributed the hydrogen bomb to the cause, and the arms race seemed to know no limits. Even while avoiding the devastation of a war that has to date never happened—World War III, that is—the Cold War ignited one diplomatic crisis after another, as well as numerous little hot wars around the world, over which hovered the threat of thermonuclear disaster. The Cold War ended, it is said, with the breakup of the Eastern Bloc, the fall of the Soviet Union, the dismantling of the Berlin Wall, and the fizzling of the arms race in the late 1980s. In the language of the day, arms always meant nuclear weaponry, first developed to end the world war, or in the idealistic view of some scientists who worked on the first bomb, the weapon to end all war (as World War I was supposedly the war to end all wars). Then in the postwar period, arms were perfected and expanded to the point that human-made Armageddon, the end of the world in a blaze of missile exchange, came to be not only imaginable but really possible for the first time in history: Mutual Assured Destruction, MADness. Various treaties hinted at the end of the Cold War before the walls fell and the Iron Curtain lifted: test ban treaties, nuclear proliferation agreements, and so on. Then, when the Soviet Union could no longer sustain itself, a victim of the economy as much as anything else—the other weaponry of modern times—the world breathed a sigh of relief. For a generation, humanity had lived in the shadow of the mushroom cloud, imagining in literature, cinema, song, and sermon what it would be like to survive the atomic blast, or fail to survive, leaving an empire of insects and grass, the only life likely to survive a global thermonuclear war (as Jonathan Schell memorably imagined the scene in *The Fate of the Earth*).

As the shadow seemed to lift, global life became a matter of living in the ruins. For, like any war, the Cold War left ruins for future generations to sort through and ponder.

As the epicenter of the bomb's historical origins, New Mexico offers an especially rich site for exploring ruins, from the Cold War and otherwise. From the geological remnants of former ages—the gorges, mesas, mountains, and lava fields—to the ceremonial kivas of Chaco Canyon and the spearpoints of Neolithic hunters lying in the dry sand of Clovis, then on to the museums and legacies of the Nuclear Age from Los Alamos in the north to Carlsbad in the south, the state welcomes the pilgrim seeking a meditation on the wonders and worries, the glories and follies of the past. The natural beauty of the place eases the pilgrim's passage: the seductive draw of the dry air, the narrow canyons and wind-sculpted rock formations, the craggy mountains, the sparkling light and desert sky—a natural playground for the hardy adventurer, an artist's outdoor studio, a photographer's and filmmaker's delight.

Nuclear New Mexico, in conjunction with natural New Mexico, beckons to the traveler in search of a fading past, a place in the present, and a future legacy for humanity and the natural environment. If that sounds good, drive on.

Trinity

The tour begins at Trinity Site, alternately celebrated as a place of beginnings or a place of endings—where the atomic bomb was first tested, where World War II discovered its endgame, or where the thing that arguably ended that war first proved possible—and where the Cold War and the Atomic Age arguably began: where everything changed. "The release of atomic power has changed everything," Albert Einstein famously said, "except our way of thinking" (quoted in Johnson, *Romancing the Atom*, xi). If not our way of thinking, though, certainly the human way of being in the world has changed since Trinity. The "original bombheads," says Don DeLillo in his novel *Underworld*, "all those émigrés from Middle Europe, thick-browed men with sad eyes and roomy pleated pants, . . . came to do science in New Mexico during the war . . . and worked on the thing that had no name, the bomb that would redefine the limits of human perception" (421–22).

The new perception centered on the "thing that had no name" (like an unapproachable god). It was called "the gadget" during the Manhattan Project at Los Alamos, mainly for security reasons (Monk, *Robert Oppenheimer*, 362). The version of the gadget tested at Trinity,

Tourists line up to enter the White Sands Missile Range, home of Trinity Site

a plutonium or implosion bomb, was supposed to include a "214-ton Thermos-shaped steel and concrete container" that did get a name, vaguely cartoonlike and mock-comical: Jumbo. It was a fitting moniker. The thing was big, after all, and the funny name deflected the scariness of the whole enterprise. Ultimately, it was not used for its original purpose—to protect the "precious plutonium core" from a misfire or failed explosion. The idea was abandoned, and Jumbo was placed within blast range of the gadget. It became part of the experiment to determine the destructive power of the explosion, which was certainly no misfire. But Jumbo survived and stands now as a setting for photo shots at the entry gate of Trinity Site ("Jumbo," Trinity Atomic Website).

Amid the prancing celebration of the gadget's success and the sigh of relief that the bomb had worked and did not (as some had feared it might) incinerate the atmosphere, Oppenheimer got it right when he later recalled thinking of words from the *Bhagavad Gita*:

> We knew that the world would not be the same. A few people laughed, a few people cried. Most people were silent. I remembered the line from the Hindu scripture, the *Bhagavad-Gita*: Vishnu is trying to persuade the Prince that he should do his duty and to impress him he takes on his multi-armed form and says, "Now I am become death, the destroyer of worlds." (quoted in Rhodes, *Making of the Atomic Bomb*, 676; see also Else, *Day after Trinity*)

The words loosely translated from the *Bhagavad Gita* have become the most famous quotation of the Atomic Age—for a reason. With the success of the atomic bomb, the awareness of human power—or the *"illusion* of unlimited power," as Frank Oppenheimer, Robert's brother, once called it (see Else, *Day after Trinity*)—increased by an order of magnitude. At times, the mood it inspires is ecstatic, fueling near worship of the Manhattan Project heroes and patriotic pride in intellectual achievement and unmatched technological glory. At other times, the mood grows dark, ridden with overwhelming guilt and anxiety, commensurate with the status that only a god species can know, the tragic god who says, "What have I done?"

Oppenheimer resorted to god language to communicate the depth of the change, and he didn't stop with the Hindu citation. He also spoke of "the legend of Prometheus," the demigod of Greek mythology who brought fire to humanity, and "the deep sense of guilt in man's new powers, that reflects his recognition of evil, and his long knowledge of it" (quoted in Rhodes, *Making of the Atomic Bomb*, 676). In naming the test site "Trinity," he foresaw the great change again in religious terms. As he explained in a letter to General Groves years later, Trinity was a reference to the religious writings of the English poet and cleric John Donne, notably the sonnet "Batter My Heart, Three-Person'd God" (Rhodes, *Making of the Atomic Bomb*, 571–72).

When the big change came, it came very fast. The weapon became reality in less than one human lifetime after the discovery of radioactivity. As one of the scientists who worked on the H-bomb at Los Alamos in the early 1950s, Kenneth Ford marvels at this rapid evolution. "When Henri Becquerel, in Paris, discovered radioactivity in 1896, my parents were pre-schoolers," Ford writes, and the "history of nuclear energy from Becquerel to bombs, from a few relatively harmless alpha, beta, and gamma rays to the destruction of cities and the obliteration of a Pacific island was accomplished in one human lifetime. In 1952, the year in which [the hydrogen bomb] 'Mike' released its ten megatons and [the island] Elugelab was no more, my parents turned sixty" (*Building the H Bomb*, 44). Since that Pacific island test, another generation, the one known as the baby boomers, has grown up and grown old in the wake of those first explosions and has struggled to fathom the difference that nuclear power has made in the life of humanity. It's been just over seventy years—three score years and ten, the life of a good man, according to the Bible—since the detonation of the first atomic bomb in 1945.

Go then to Trinity Site. Here the fate of the earth appeared in the vision (literal and prophetic) of a few men, military and scientific, in the predawn air of Tularosa Basin between the Oscura Mountains to

Entrance to Trinity Site

the east, the San Mateos and Magdalenas on the western horizon, and the Rio Grande (well before it turns southeastward and becomes the US-Mexico border) running in its north-south rift some ten miles to the west. Here the sun rose twice in this desert land on the morning of July 16, 1945; in the darkness before dawn, the iconic mushroom cloud climbed out of its fireball shell into the sky for the first time; and Dr. Oppenheimer strutted in his famous porkpie hat as the Manhattan Project proved its value to the military cause and science came to matter as never before. The light-stepping Oppenheimer from the old films at Trinity Site, virtually dancing with excitement, later became the chastened one with large sad eyes, pensively sucking his pipe and solemnly wearing his uniform of academic tweeds, bearing the burden of a world that first celebrated, then reviled and dismissed him—the very embodiment, whether elevated or brought low, of the scientific ego in modern times. (Was his death from throat cancer caused by tobacco or radiation exposure? In his prime, we fully understood neither danger.)

Trinity Site

As he celebrated his great success at Trinity, the fallout rained on the backs of cattle, ranch cats, pronghorns, and jackrabbits, the detritus of the gadget. Falling from a tower at ground zero to discharge an unparalleled show of destructive potential, the gadget was only an *experiment* in one sense, but it was also the ultimate *experience* of modern humanity.

Now the place seems almost inconsequential. Now, as then (except for the few moments of the blast), most visitors to Trinity Site would say that there's really not that much to see. Then again, there's everything. It's all in the attitude.

You might arrive around Easter time. In the modernist spring, nature breeds lilacs out of the dead ground, as T. S. Eliot would say, a voice from the wasteland of World War I that chants what seems in retrospect the prophetic song of the Atomic Age. Or perhaps your poetic tastes run to the sunnier medieval outlook of Chaucer, the old author who told the tales of springtime pilgrims. After all, with its swords and sorcery, magic and menace, medievalism would become the default destination of the fantasy literature and apocalyptic visions so common in the era of the atom, from J. R. R. Tolkien, who produced his masterpiece *The Lord of the Rings* in the postwar years—with the magic ring of power providing a choice metaphor for the atomic bomb—to the more recent George R. R. Martin, author of *Game of Thrones*, who lives in Santa Fe. Back in the real Middle Ages, Chaucer saw spring as the season when folks long to go on pilgrimages. April ("the cruelest month," as Eliot says in *The Wasteland*) was for a short while the only time of year that Trinity Site was open to the public; budget cuts were cited as the reason for reducing two openings to one. With the demands of nuclear tourism, it's again open twice a year, once in spring and again in fall, the seasons of transition. Take your choice, and drive on.

You can follow the cars—a surprising number in this rural place, distant even today from large centers of population, some hundred miles south of Albuquerque, and nearly two hundred north of the El Paso/Juárez metroplex—amid huge expanses of grassland and mountains, basin and range to the west and east. You enter the gate at Stallion Site on the north side of the White Sands Missile Range; the army lieutenant checks your picture ID and gives the rules: no taking pictures or stopping on the road to Trinity Site; photos are permitted at the site, but not among the secret installations on the way; no "sit-ins or demonstrations"—his exact words, repeated in the brochure handed to you, in language you thought had gone out of use in 1975 with the end of the war in Vietnam—no collecting trinitite, the rock invented by the bomb, sand fused into a greenish glass, still mildly radioactive.

A caravan of cars arrives
at Trinity Site

Follow the line of cars to a gravel parking lot. The military police will guide you to an open spot. It might remind you of a theme
park, with shuttles lined up to carry those interested to the McDonald Ranch, land seized long ago by the federals for their mighty work.
Old Dave McDonald was compensated handsomely but was never
fully reconciled to the deal. Families unload for an add-on to their
spring break trip.

You may have wondered on the way, who comes to Trinity Site?
The answer is *everybody*—old and young, white and various shades
of brown, civilian and military, veteran and activist, working people,
and the professional classes (judging from eavesdropped accents, ru-

Warning against collecting trinitite

brics on T-shirts, and patches on vests and shoulders), with license plates from Ontario to Alabama, California to New York.

Sometimes there are special groups, like the Japanese monks who came on the sixtieth anniversary of the bombing of Hiroshima. For sixty years they had kept alive burning embers from the destruction of Hiroshima and Nagasaki, walking them back and forth between the two cities. Then they decided the time had come to lay the embers to rest. But rather than Hiroshima, they chose Trinity for the burial site. They recognized it as a point of origin, on a par with indigenous stories about places of emergence and the original life of people on the earth (see Weigle and White, *Lore of New Mexico*). Here is the place where the atomic human emerged, burdened with the knowledge of the atom's secrets and the power to destroy whole cities at a single blow. The Japanese monks received a rare dispensation to enter the site on the proper anniversary, accompanied by a delegation that included representatives of the former superpowers, Russian and US, and an interfaith group of solemn pilgrims. Everyone gathered in nearby Socorro. On August 6, 2005, the monks, who had landed in San Francisco and walked to New Mexico, buried the embers at ground zero of the old blast. A member of the delegation, Alan Wagman, wrote a commemorative poem called "A Shallow Depression." Every pilgrimage has its poets, and anniversaries always strike special chords. Wagman distributed his poem via an August 7 email to participants in a 2015 vigil at Los Alamos commemorating the seventieth anniversary of the bomb.

At the gate that opens onto the walkway leading to the site itself, the feeling suggests a rodeo, county fair, or powwow—a feature of pilgrimages from time immemorial (see Reader, *Pilgrimage*). The hucksters line up serving burgers

Tourists line up to buy T-shirts and hats at Trinity Site

A tourist poses with Jumbo at Trinity Site

Walking from the parking lot to Ground Zero

and tamales, souvenirs, T-shirts bearing nostalgic slogans with their weak humor: "Trinity Site: Duck and Cover." If you grew up in Los Alamos in the 1950s, or even a place like Houston, with refineries and oil storage units nearby, a fine target for missiles from abroad, you may have actually practiced the duck-and-cover drill in your grade school. If you grew up a little later or lived in a noncritical neighborhood, you would have missed the action and may have laughed at the old black-and-white footage of schoolchildren ducking in unison under desks that, if actually attacked by thermonuclear devices, would have incinerated in a flash.

In the midst of the holiday crowd stands a great rusty hulk, hollowed out like a big culvert, the kind that directs water under a superhighway. "All that remains of Jumbo," the sign says, indicating the

Waiting in line to pose with the Ground Zero monument

mightiest shell casing ever left at the scene of a crime, enormous and immobile, perhaps still radioactive to some degree. Yet people take turns having their pictures taken in the opening, with room enough to stand inside the thing that seems no longer ominous (right?).

There are no official photographs today, no guided tours, no speeches. The place and the artifacts are left in silence. Visitors must make of them what they can.

Leave the people lining up for the photo op at Jumbo's remains and follow the pilgrims inside the gate to walk the quarter mile to ground zero. You arrive at a depression in the plateau, maybe fifty yards wide. It's the gadget's shallow crater, you realize, the edges smoothed by the intervening years, the short yellow prairie grass partially regrown, though stamped down by the feet of the pilgrims, a chain-link fence encircling the site. Here is the "shallow depression" of Alan Wagman's poem. The phrase resonates with the mood as well as the landscape of the poem—a shallow depression standing perhaps as the psychological legacy of the Atomic Age: a numbness emanating from the blunted perception of the old reality. The bomb really exploded here, a nearly unfathomable truth.

In the center of the site stands a memorial obelisk made of green-ish-black lava rock, placed by the army in 1965, the twentieth anniversary of the explosion. Another photo op, and the people stand in line. One guy sniffs the monument with a digital Geiger counter.

Now circumnavigate the fence. Walk it like a pilgrim walks a labyrinth. On the north side hangs a series of professional photographs, set out for the biannual opening. They show soldiers lounging in the area in the days before Trinity, some swimming in the cattle tank of the McDonald Ranch, then on the day itself, the bomb exploding in stages captured by ultraslow photography. The fireball rises like the sun from a billow of dust before hatching the mushroom cloud; the project director gives an interview in the aftermath of the test; a soldier stands beside the rebar and concrete fragments of the footings that constitute the meager remainder of the gadget's tower. You look back and see the little fence that now encircles the same ruin of the

Observing the historical photographs on the fence surrounding Trinity Site

Looking for trinitite

former tower, no bigger than the sapling you might have planted in your yard last fall with chicken wire around it to keep the rabbits off. You may have seen a photo, included in Richard Rhodes's *The Making of the Atomic Bomb* and hanging on the wall of Albuquerque's National Museum of Nuclear Science and History, depicting General Groves and Dr. Oppenheimer standing over the same little ruin in the aftermath of Trinity, giants from the land of history casually conversing over the destruction they've wreaked.

Leave the pictures on the fence and stroll to the center of the crater. On a truck trailer is a bomb casing like the one dropped on Hiroshima, apparently pulled onto the site for the spring event. Some lads are goofing off, and one climbs aboard and straddles the device in imitation of the famous ride of Slim Pickens's character in *Dr. Strangelove*. The boy even wears a cowboy hat like old Slim's. Has he planned ahead for this moment, a vacation in iconicity?

Somebody finds a tiny sliver of trinitite, and people gather around to stare. You hold it for a moment, then give it back, absently wiping your hand on your pants (as if the habitual gesture might erase the exposure). A young woman comes over with a Geiger counter. You leave before the reading.

Follow the pilgrims back to the parking lot, get in the car, drive back the way you came, and you might see a pair of pronghorns grazing alongside the government road.

A sign at the intersection where the government road leading out of Stallion Site meets US Highway 380 points south and says "Trinitite for Sale: 8.5 Miles." It's worth the detour to go 8.5 miles south on 380 to the rock shop in Bingham, New Mexico, which stands at the intersection of the dirt road that leads out to the old Blanchard Mine. The shop is the only building left in the village. The husband of the current owner will tell you that in this remote location, the day Trinity Site is open is the busiest and most lucrative of the year, so he's never actually seen the site. If you've been coming here for thirty years or more, this day is probably the only time you've seen more than a car or two in the parking lot. Now it's swarming with nuclear tourists,

(overleaf) Trinitite

Trinitite
for sale

mainly families with kids out to augment a rock collection. If you were here as late as the 1980s, you'll remember the previous owner, the colorful Sam Jones, known as Rattlesnake Sam. He kept a pit full of serpents in front of the shop, which he said he collected for scientists in Colorado. For a while, he also had a big cage of bobcats in back of the place. He led tours up to the old mine, for which he was the caretaker, wearing a sidearm and cowboy hat, a stogie perpetually stuck in his jaw.

These days you can stand by the circular spot where the snake pit used to be, now filled in, and look up toward the foothills of the Oscura, your eyes seeking the ledge in front of the mine, and you remember the great steel door that Sam would open with a creak to expose the walls to the sunlight that would gleam brightly on the galena crystals still intact. If you stepped too close to the edge of that ledge out front, surveying the basin below for signs of Trinity Site,

Trinitite prices

Sam would pull you back with a flourish and tell you dramatically how an unexpected gust of wind once carried a man right over the lip of that cliff. Sam died in 1992, though his wife, Vera, lived on until just recently, the current owner will tell you.

Here you can buy fluorite and galena crystals taken from the mine, which once yielded a profitable load of barite and lead ore, maybe even some silver and gold. You can buy other rare and local rocks like smithsonite and fire agate—five to six dollars a carat. More expensive yet are the samples of trinitite, which you can purchase before returning to Socorro for the night, where other natural wonders await in the land of the Rio Grande Rift.

Bosque del Apache

Less than an hour's drive northwest, you can be back in Socorro. The town's name derives from the succor that the Spanish found there after traversing the cart-friendly but fatally dry shortcut along the Rio Grande Rift northward from Las Cruces, the fabled Jornada del Muerto, or Day's March of the Dead One. "The grim suitability of this place name [for the siting of Trinity] could not have been lost on the ironic and poetic genius of Dr. J. Robert Oppenheimer," says the Rio Grande historian Paul Horgan (*Great River*, ix). In Socorro, the local Piro Pueblo Indians introduced the conquistadors and friars to the reliable spring at the foot of the mountain before later driving the colonists away during the Pueblo Revolt. Living water from the same spring now greens the golf course and campus of the New Mexico Institute of Mining and Technology, formerly the School of Mines—hence the *M* on the mountain there, repainted by freshmen every year. You can check into your motel, take a siesta, then in late afternoon head south again to the Bosque del Apache National Wildlife Refuge, ten miles from the village of San Antonio, where you can fortify yourself with a "world famous" green chili cheeseburger at the Owl Bar and Grill (unless the day of contemplating bombs and radioactive exposure, or some scruple like vegetarianism, limits your appetite).

In recent times the Owl has been challenged by the only other eating and drinking establishment in the village of San Antonio, the up-start Buckhorn Tavern, which has somehow become the darling of the guidebooks and travel magazines. But the one boast of the Owl that the Buckhorn will never match is the historical connection with Nuclear New Mexico. In an effort to capitalize on the new wave of nuclear tourism, a flyer is displayed in every booth that tells how returning war vet Frank Chavez opened the Owl early in 1945. Soon after, a handful of self-proclaimed "prospectors" from a nearby gov-

The wetlands of Bosque del Apache National Wildlife Refuge.
Trinity Site is just this side of the mountain ridge in the distance.

History flyer displayed
at the Owl Bar and Grill

ernment installation made the place their hangout: "These 'prospectors' were actually atomic scientists who would activate the famous Trinity Site explosion, the first test of the atom bomb used to end the war with its devastation of two Japanese cities." According to the flyer, it was the Trinity scientists who originally talked Frank into adding a grill to the bar, where he began to cook the green chili cheeseburger; the recipe allegedly "remains unchanged since 1948." Frank's daughter and her husband still operate the Owl Bar and Grill, where you can have locally ground beef and good chili with a side of history. Then drive on for the nature tour.

Inside the Owl Bar and Grill

The Bosque is a series of fields, shallow marshes, and cottonwood groves where the Rio Grande slows down and widens out. In the winter, the fields fill with literally thousands of snow geese and sandhill cranes; they will have fled north to their summering grounds in Canada by the time Trinity Site opens in the spring, but will have returned by the October opening.

Even in April, the Bosque rarely fails to offer something good to see. You may spot a remnant flight of the white geese over one of the ponds on the South Tour. Walk the paths there, and after passing the signs that warn of mountain lions in the area, you may catch a view of bachelor wild turkeys practicing their displays for the mating season. Back in the car, on the North Tour, you could come upon a strange gathering of a dozen or so northern harriers of all ages and genders, acting more like chickens than hawks, strutting around in the field. You can puzzle over the phenomenon with other visitors who raise their binoculars and enormous telephoto lenses to gaze on the scene. On the way out, you may see a raven trying to wedge its horny bill into the carapace of a turtle—to get the last morsel of meat, you wonder, or reach the first bite of the creature withdrawn deep into its

Moonrise over
Bosque del Apache

A snow goose falls prey to a coyote

Tourists with cameras,
Bosque del Apache

shell? The determined pecking and prying of the great bird leave little hope for the turtle's survival.

You drive out, perhaps remembering the ponds on the outskirts of the refuge from a winter visit, teeming with cranes and geese. The ground and sky in your memory swirl with activity.

You could think about how global climate change is said to have altered the migratory patterns of birds and other animals. There are javelina (collared peccaries) in the Bosque now and birds like the pyrrhuloxia (Mexican cardinal), which never used to come this far north. The range maps of birding guidebooks over ten years old are outdated by climate change.

Recalling the proximity of the missile range to the east, almost forgotten in the reverie on nature that the Bosque inspires, you may remember the concept of nuclear winter—the theory of what would happen if a thermonuclear disaster raised a pall of dust into the atmosphere, thick and extensive enough to lower the temperature of the earth for decades, spoiling the growing season of temperate climes and leading to worldwide famine. Would the cranes and geese still come here, to these fields where millet and corn are now planted for

Javelina crossing Highway 1 near the Bosque del Apache National Wildlife Refuge

them, if all that remains are the grasses that grow in the marshes, where the Apache hunting parties once camped in the groves by the river on trips down from Sierra Blanca in the mountains east of the site, now occupied by the missile range?

You may be thinking of how the wide-ranging actions of the human race change the ancient patterns of movement and circulation of resources and life forms—of water, insects, animals, native people, and plants. And of how Jonathan Schell, who wrote the bestseller *The Fate of the Earth* in the waning years of the Cold War, has said in his latest (and lesser known) book that the nuclear threat forms an interesting comparison to global climate change—"the only other catastrophe on the horizon whose consequences are in the same league with a nuclear holocaust."

The two perils . . . are [both] the fruit of swollen human power—in the one case, the destructive power of war; in the other, the productive power of fossil-fuel energy. . . . Both threaten life on a planetary scale. Both require a fully global response. Anyone concerned by the one should be concerned with the other. It would be a shame to save the Earth from slowly warming only to burn it up in an instant in a nuclear war. (*Seventh Decade*, 7–8)

But there's a crucial difference, in Schell's view. The interest in global warming waxes in the public mind, while attention to nuclear issues wanes. The nuclear dilemma, he says, "tends to circumvent ordinary mechanisms of response to danger," while global warming "has conformed to a pattern that is familiar from other gathering dangers, such as the AIDS epidemic or the threat to the ozone layer from man-made chemicals." The pattern goes like this:

First, the peril appears and is disclosed to the world in specialized journals and to a certain extent in the press but is largely ignored by politicians and the public. Then the evidence grows, and alarm increases. As the predictions begin to come true, frightening reading material is supplemented by disturbing concrete experiences. In the case of global warming, these have included hotter summers, more frequent and more powerful hurricanes, rising sea levels, more flooding in low-lying areas and more drought elsewhere, vanishing species, disintegrating coral reefs, and melting glaciers and polar ice. Photographic evidence becomes available, and the problem can be shown on television—or made into a film, such as former vice president Al Gore's *An Inconvenient Truth*. Apathy and denial now have a potent competitor in the pressure of events. The question, complex in practice but simple in principle, becomes whether the unpleasant initial consequences can inspire political action fast enough to head off utter calamity later on. (*Seventh Decade*, 7–8)

You may doubt Schell's optimism about the progress of recognizing the truth of global climate change. You may feel that it is still largely subject to denial, distraction, and defensiveness, and victimized by the political will of the oil companies and extractive industries and their paid servants in the government (see Killingsworth, *Facing It*). Or you may feel that the human contribution to global warming is overstated; that the whole business is part of a great natural cycle. But as a point of contrast to the nuclear question, although the threat of rogue nations like North Korea and Iran and the competition for more and more countries to become "nuclear nations" has grown since he published his book in 2007, many of Schell's observations still ring true:

> No such sequence [of recognition and response] has been exhibited in the evolution of the nuclear danger. The most important reason is that the transition from warning to experience has not—most fortunately—occurred. No nuclear weapon has been exploded in anger since the destruction of Nagasaki on August 9, 1945. Instead, a welcome if tenuous "tradition of nonuse" has developed. To be sure, the worldwide buildup of the machinery of nuclear power and nuclear war has exacted a significant medical and environmental price. The fallout from nuclear tests has caused a worldwide increase in deaths from cancer. The Chernobyl disaster of 1986, in which a nuclear power plant exploded in Ukraine, contaminated several hundred square miles of the surrounding territory with radiation. Nuclear wastes from both nuclear weapons production and nuclear plants, some of which will remain radioactive for as long as a million years, are heaping up around the world, and no one is certain what to do with them over the long run. However, grave as these costs may be, they obviously have not had the overwhelming impact on the public mind that would be produced by the sudden, colossal devastation of a nuclear war, which continues to hide its face. (*Seventh Decade*, 8–9)

Spaceport America

Leaving the Bosque del Apache, some tourists choose to drive south on I-25 rather than return to Socorro for the night. You pass through chili country in a region that alternates between wilderness and sparse settlement, with settlement devoted to both agriculture and high-tech adventure, a zone famous for rockets and missiles, from a time when the Space Age and the Atomic Age overlapped, one helping to define the other.

You might consider stopping at the relatively new Spaceport America (although check first or book a tour online or at the Spaceport America Visitor Center in the town of Truth or Consequences [T or C], as the secure facility requires tickets for access and is often closed to tourists). Situated on a large tract of desert land between Truth or Consequences and Las Cruces and bordering the White Sands Missile Range, it boasts the first commercially based launching pad for space-bound rockets, for both research and, ultimately, public transportation. It also leases facilities to filmmakers, corporations, educators, government contractors, and others for special events such as the June 2017 Spaceport America Cup, "the world's largest rocket engineering competition . . . [for] university students from six continents . . . to design and build rockets" ("Rocket Fever," 2017). It may be a while, however, before you can book a half-hour coast-to-coast or hour-long worldwide suborbital flight, even though such public transportation venues are in already in the planning stages.

Alamogordo

After taking a nice long soak in one of the many hot springs in T or C,[1] you might make another stop on the missile-and-rocket subtour at Alamogordo, east of I-25 on Highway 70, home of Holloman Air Force Base and gateway to both the White Sands Missile Range and White Sands National Monument. Once again, there is the seemingly inevitable pairing of a natural attraction with a military installation. Like most of the state's many military sites, the missile range is off limits to tourists except during the opening of Trinity Site. You can, however, visit the Missile Range Museum, the New Mexico Museum of Space History, or the International Space Hall of Fame, all a part of the technological legacy of Nuclear New Mexico and the ensuing Space Age. The arms race was mirrored during the Cold War by the space race.

But most visitors will tell you that White Sands National Monument, the local taste of the natural world untouched by agriculture or industry, is the big attraction in the Alamogordo area. Your first view of the national monument's gypsum sands, bleached blindingly white by a sun that shines 350 days a year in this blanched land, is startling. If you have youngsters with you, allow some time to tumble or slide down the dunes. Be sure to wear dark shades if you plan to walk or jog the Park Service roads, where you can learn firsthand about the phenomenon of mirage and natural hallucination in the region of the Jornada del Muerto.

1. The town of Truth or Consequences was once named Hot Springs. It changed its name in 1950 as part of a promotional scheme for the radio program *Truth or Consequences*. The host Ralph Edwards offered to broadcast his tenth-anniversary show from any town that would change its name to the name of the program. Hot Springs accepted the challenge. Most people in New Mexico call it "T or C."

Carlsbad

From Alamogordo, you can take Highway 82 to Artesia and then head south on US 285 to the next stop on the tour, Carlsbad, which hosts another pair of attractions from Nuclear and Natural New Mexico: the Waste Isolation Pilot Plant, or WIPP site, just east of town, and Carlsbad Caverns, to the west. Consider first the WIPP site, a place whose very design seems to hurry the waning of interest in nuclear matters that Jonathan Schell worried over in his 2007 book.

The road to WIPP

Waste Isolation Pilot Plant

If the Cold War begins at Trinity Site, it ends at the WIPP site, at least if you follow the drift of the public-relations messages coming out of the Department of Energy (DOE). The DOE office for the WIPP site lies west of Carlsbad on National Park Highway. There the government greets its public. Admission to the actual site (in the other direction, east of Carlsbad) is, of course, restricted.

But you are welcome in the lobby of the office, where your DOE hosts provide a virtual tour under the watchful eyes of friendly security officers who will call the public relations (PR) liaison to come out and interact with you, the public. The lobby of the building is a little museum of pictorial displays and placards on tripods with explanations and images of the mine-like facility in the deep salt beds of the Permian Basin. If you come in April, close to Earth Day, you may find an encouraging display of earth-friendly practices undertaken by the DOE staff. You'll be invited to watch a short video. You'll be handed brochures (*The WIPP Experience: Benefits to the Nation* and *WIPP: The Waste Isolation Pilot Plant*). You'll be able to take home a sample of NaCl crystals in a little plastic envelope that says

> Permian Age Rock Salt
> 250 million years old
> From the 2,150 ft.
> Underground disposal level
> Waste Isolation Pilot Plant (WIPP)
> East of Carlsbad, New Mexico
> US Department of Energy
> Carlsbad Field Office
> 1–800–336–WIPP
> (1–800–336–9477)
> www.wipp.energy.gov

The sample suggests the odd mixture of open and closed access. The information is all yours, nothing to hide, fascinating in the way of natural history everywhere (millions of years old—hinting at stability—and safe as table salt), but it's still *out there* (east of Carlsbad) and you are *over here* (west of town).

Waste Isolation Pilot Plant

If you show interest and hint that you're a writer or researcher, the PR liaison will say you may be able to visit the actual site if you get a clearance after undergoing a background check in advance. She may give you a bigger chunk of salt if one happens to be on hand, and let you have a copy of the DVD shown on the little TV set in the lobby.

The film, like the brochure, is titled *The WIPP Experience*. It says *experience* rather than *experiment*, despite the word *pilot* in the name of the place, which implies an experimental and provisional arrangement. But *experience* connotes something that lasts, that has a story, that involves people, that is as familiar as table salt: everybody has *experiences*, while only scientists, with their image problems in the public eye, do *experiments*.

The film tells about the kind of depository that WIPP is—a sort of reverse mine, where things are put into the earth rather than taken out. The deep salt deposit allegedly has the virtue of sealing whatever is placed inside it. The film gives the rough outlines of WIPP's history and explains the variety of waste deposited there: transuranic materials irradiated during research and development, often things as mundane and unthreatening as lab equipment and clothes exposed to radiation at government facilities, *not* high-level waste produced in weapons manufacture and *not* waste generated by power plants, all of which must still be stored on site at the place of production. You may have heard elsewhere that because on-site storage facilities are pressed to the limit, plans are underway to expand the mission of WIPP to include these more ominous wastes. The plan faces the same kind of uphill battle that occurred at the proposed high-level waste site at Yucca Mountain, Nevada, which met strong resistance from both casino owners ninety miles away in Las Vegas and local Indian tribes, the Shoshone and the Paiute (see Kuletz, *Tainted Desert*). It's now become a political football, as President Obama removed the project's funding and President Trump (as of this writing) has vowed to restore it (see YuccaMountain.org). You also may have heard early reports that nuclear science and engineering are on the verge of perfecting a method that will render nuclear waste harmless. But for now, the waste remains a worrisome problem.

You'd never know it from the film playing at the WIPP office. It is anything but ominous and makes no promises about the future. Its main points are that WIPP is *safe*. The word and its variants (*safety*, *safely*, etc.) are repeated over and over, always with a not-so-subtle emphasis and slight increase in pitch and volume in the voice of the narrator.

The film contrasts strongly with other depictions of waste sites. In Don DeLillo's novel *Underworld*, for example, a fictitious waste disposal specialist visits a similar (but also fictitious) experimental facility in salt beds on the Texas Gulf Coast. He speaks of the burial deep underground in tones of reverence. Waste experts don the mantle of the priest who buries the dangerous remains of the dead. The narrator says,

> [We] watched men in moon suits bury drums of dangerous waste in subterranean salt beds many millions of years old, dried-out remnants of a Mesozoic ocean. It was a religious conviction in our business that these deposits of rock salt would not leak radiation. Waste is a religious thing. We entomb contaminated waste with a sense of reverence and dread. It is necessary to respect what we discard. (88)

But the PR rhetoric at WIPP has no truck with reverence, respect, and dread—attitudes that could undermine the hard-won claims of safety. Instead, the film and brochures are inclined to trivialize the operation. Rather than ritual, it's routine. No magic is needed, no priestcraft, no blessings and prayers, which would, after all, imply the presence of witchery, not the science that has gone before. There's nothing to it. Forget about it.

Slightly subtler is the rhetorical use of history. The waste, says the film narrator, is often "Cold War–era" refuse. The implication is that once the Cold War ended, somebody had to clean up. Facilities in places like Los Alamos, Oak Ridge, Hanford, and Aiken (South Carolina) generated a great deal of radioactive garbage during the arms race. What was needed was a remote garbage dump where it could be removed from the original facilities and *safely* deposited more or less forever. The film suggests that the waste is history; it has no *presence*: it is not *present* in either the physical sense of *here* or the temporal sense of *now*. Like the Soviet Union, it is gone. The world is a *safer* place without it (the waste and the USSR). Forget about it. It's gone.

But, of course, it's not gone. In February 2014, independent monitors in the Carlsbad area detected traces of airborne plutonium and americium. Officials at WIPP revealed that a leak had occurred in one of the storage tunnels. Eventually it came out that a number of workers had been exposed and placed under observation. The low levels of radiation that leaked into the atmosphere posed no threat to the general public, the officials declared. But the project was shut down. Plans to begin accepting high-level waste at WIPP—plans not mentioned in the PR—were put on hold. Even shipments of the usual low-level stuff had to be delayed indefinitely. Officials such as US senator Tom Udall (D-New Mexico) worried publicly about materials ready for shipment that had to remain on the mesa at Los Alamos (see Clausing, "Leaks, Accidents").

It doesn't take much of a threat to unbalance stability and undermine safety when radioactivity is involved. Despite the claims of safety, most folks find the stuff just plain scary. And yet there was never any serious opposition to WIPP down in the Carlsbad region. As one resident told Eric L. Morgan, a scholar who specializes in the political rhetoric of Nuclear New Mexico, "the people wanted it. Ever since oil and gas went bust, it's hard to stay in the area" ("Regional Communication," 122). Oil and gas have come back since then, as any drive through the apocalyptic landscape east of Artesia will affirm, a scene straight out of a science fiction film about mining the asteroids or some other desolate place.[2] Another of Morgan's informants disagreed about the economic reasoning while agreeing on the lack of opposition to WIPP: "Well, now, oil and gas money was never really Carlsbad. Most of the oil and gas was in Artesia . . . and Hobbs, and even Lovington some, but Carlsbad was always potash" (124). Potash is a mineral used in fertilizer. The production of fertilizer has always been big in Carlsbad, beginning perhaps with the mining of bat guano in Carlsbad Caverns. But fertilizer never commanded the economic power of the fuel industry. As Morgan notes, "there's always been a rivalry between Artesia and Carlsbad," with Carlsbad typically characterized "as being bigger, and thus more politically powerful, but also more impoverished" (124).

Carlsbad Caverns

From the Department of Energy Office on the outskirts of Carlsbad, you can continue driving west (away from the waste) out National Park Highway to Carlsbad Caverns—the place of natural beauty that forms the seemingly inevitable counterpoint to the Atomic Age WIPP site on the tour of Nuclear New Mexico. The old billboards lead the way—fifties-era affairs, the images fading, left as they are, presumably because of nostalgia if not tight budgets.

If you are of a certain age, one of the baby boomers, the sons and daughters of the Atomic Age, you will certainly feel it, the creeping nostalgia overtaking you. Even the Cold War feels nostalgic for boomers. Nostalgia settles in the sanitized memory of the 1950s. *Leave It to Beaver, Father Knows Best*—the fifties were nostalgic even in the fifties, it seems, harking back to some golden age that the TV producers were trying to pass off as existing in the present, as having *presence*.

You may well remember the old days at the caverns, the era depicted by the billboards, as you descend into the gloom on the concrete trail (with minimal lighting to protect the extraordinary formations), past structures that were born in the dark and to the dark

2. At the time of this writing, that is. Since then, oil has plummeted again. Warning: The landscape of Nuclear New Mexico is a shifting scene, sometimes dizzying to travel.

National Park
Highway
to Carlsbad
Caverns

The Apache
Canyon Trading
Post roadside
attraction on
the National
Park Highway
to Carlsbad
Caverns

Entrance to Carlsbad Caverns

of the underground remain unique—stalactites, stalagmites, glistening mineral-made icicles and hanging sheets. The variety stands in strong contrast to what the images of the WIPP underground site convey, massive deposits of nothing but salt.

You may try to recover the amazement of your first childhood visit, but forget it. What's missing? The color, of course! Back in the fifties and early sixties, the caverns were not so black and white (with only a splash of color here or there, like a mistake or a faulty setting on the old TVs). Unlike the TV back then, the caverns were in full color, like reality. Your memory says the color was part of the amazing natural formations, a separate underground reality, the lurid pinks and alien greens and neon blues. But your memory is mistaken. You know now that the color came from filtered lights set up to augment touristic amazement. That kind of lighting had to be removed and the overall lighting subdued and subjected to periodic shifts after the National Park staff came to realize that the lights were damaging the place, causing algae to grow that would eat away at the formations.

Trail through Carlsbad Caverns

Concession stand in
Carlsbad Caverns

(*below*) Oilfields and WIPP

The place wanted darkness to sustain itself, to grow its ghostly calcium, to let the water drip and solidify like hot underground ice, like nuclear winter.

Your calf muscles cramp on the steep path and you fight off disappointment, knowing that things in the caverns are better now, more attuned to the needs of nature. You can amuse yourself by inventing alternate names to replace the epic and fantastic titles given in the old days to the temples, towers, and castles of calcium. Call that one the sweet potato, this one the mattress of spines, that one over there the precancerous polyps in the intestines of the earth.

You're hungry, but the restaurant in the grand cavern at the end of the trail, the one advertised on the old billboards—"Dine thousands of feet underground!"—has been permanently closed, the operation having apparently interfered with the flight of bats through the caverns (Harden, "Deep in Carlsbad Cave").[3] So crowd onto the elevator with the other tourists and ride back to the surface. Leave it all be-

3. Not only is the area a major flyway for bats entering and exiting the cavern, but the odors apparently also attracted rodents and other living creatures not native to the area. While there are still dimly lit picnic tables available, as well as a few vending machines, for a full-service meal, you'll have to go topside.

THE HISTORICAL TOUR

hind like the Cold War buried in the grand caverns of salt some forty miles eastward. Fight off the feeling that nostalgia—the feeling that the Australian ecopsychologist Glenn Albrecht calls "solastalgia,"— threatens to become not the melancholy or homesickness that arises from a sense of a lost time or place, but the melancholy or homesickness felt in a familiar place, right there at home.

Eat a quesadilla in the visitor center café. The chilies are surprisingly tasty. The desert outside the window, the old aboveground world, is starting to bloom; the red tips of the ocotillos gleam like firebrands in the bright sun. Here the color is truly living.

Was it the WIPP experience that made the underground world feel violated and yet routine or desolate, lacking in human interest? Did it make you want to say "how beautiful" or "amazing" and then hurry away?

Don't go there. Get back in the car and keep driving.

Los Alamos

After a decade of delays and resistance, WIPP won final approval in 1992, following the end of the Cold War, a legacy it worked to erase. It did not receive its first shipment of waste until 1999. But as early as 1989, arguably the year the Cold War ended, WIPP was a done deal.

The project's approval may have depended more on the building of a road in northern New Mexico than on the fall of the Soviet Union or the approval of the people and the condition of the land in the Carlsbad region. According to Eric Morgan, the opposition to WIPP centered in the capital city of Santa Fe, and "most people [there] didn't really care about southeastern New Mexico. Rather, they were more interested in the potential disaster of trucks with TRU-PACT containers barreling down St. Francis Drive . . . , carrying deadly nuclear waste from that den of secrecy twenty minutes northwest known as Los Alamos. That concern was alleviated with the opening of a by-

A distant view of
Los Alamos National
Laboratory from the
corner of Trinity and
Oppenheimer

Statues of Oppenheimer and Groves in front of the Fuller Lodge

pass (NM 599)," also known as "the Santa Fe Relief Route" ("Regional Communication," 115–16).

If you lived near Santa Fe during the heat of the controversy, you might have seen bumper stickers like the one that said SPLIT WOOD, NOT ATOMS. The slogan seems ironic in hindsight, after the dawning of public awareness about global climate change and the understanding that carbon as well as radiation could lead to atmospheric disaster. But the slogan and other means of campaigning must have worked at the time, for the opposition got what it wanted. The road was built. Now the trucks skim along the western outskirts of the city, like the waste in the salt beds for which they are destined: out of sight and out of mind.

Some people who live in New Mexico appreciate Highway 599 for reasons other than the peace of mind it allows the residents of Santa Fe. It lets you get from Albuquerque to points north like Española and Taos without having to slog through the traffic of the capital city—where, by tourism standards, there's a whole lot of something going on.

The tour you're on today takes the bypass to another locale: Los Alamos, the place that General Groves and Dr. Oppenheimer selected to build the secret wartime city to become headquarters for the Manhattan Project, where the atomic bomb was designed and constructed. Back then, Los Alamos was little more than a muddy military outpost for most of its inhabitants. Now it's a sprawling facility with tall modern buildings that are easily visible from the road. The National Lab consists of even more areas that are not visible from your drive.

Los Alamos National Laboratory

Like the city of Los Alamos, Los Alamos National Laboratory (LANL) is situated on the stunningly beautiful Pajarito Plateau, bisected by a series of deep canyons spanned by only a few bridges (often resulting in much backtracking to get from point A to point B). Even if you try to bypass LANL, you may inadvertently find yourself in a long line of cars that split into multiple lanes, each passing a security booth,

THE HISTORICAL TOUR

Security entrance to LANL

where you will be told by a uniformed officer that security clearance is required for admission. The guard will tell you how to turn your car around and go elsewhere.

While the lab was initially created as a secret facility designed to serve as a research and development center, drawing scientists and engineers (and their families) from all over the world to work on the atomic bomb, its current mission as posted on its website is to "solve national security challenges through scientific excellence." The lab is engaged in such obvious areas as exploration of the constantly revised structure of the atom via particle physics, radiation exposure and storage, astrophysics, satellite imaging, space weather, and weapons technology (among other areas of scientific expertise). The research and development (R&D) areas have been broadened to include medical health issues (such as nanotechnologies and cell biology, including biohazards and cancer—sometimes directly related to radiation exposure), solar power and other alternative fuels, climate change and its effect on forest health, mining technologies, hydrology, magnetics, statistics, and just about every other cutting-edge scientific topic you can imagine (including the possibility of alien life). Much of the research in these new areas of specialization has earned wide recognition and is considered world class.

R&D is carried out not only in the main lab facility, but in numerous areas on smaller plateaus accessible from one of only three roads entering and leaving the plateau. Most areas are not visible from the road and are typically labeled by signs stating simply "Area X," where "X" is a number. (The labels uncomfortably recall the infamous Area 51 from UFO movies, TV shows, and popular culture publications, the Nevada site where aliens were allegedly kept after the supposed Roswell crash of 1947.) As you drive along the road, you may also notice warning signs indicating the possible presence of buried land mines, apparently left from the Cold War era. Whether true or not, the signs definitely deter hiking in this scenic secured area. There are *not* signs indicating the very real presence of nuclear waste-storage facilities scattered amid the deep canyons.

Back in the 1980s, the lab was somewhat more accessible. You might have participated in a summer teacher-training workshop at LANL that took a small group of educators to some of the more benign R&D areas, including one focused on solar panel production, one on materials science, and another on pine beetles (an infestation at that time was decimating the local forests). One session introduced teachers to scientific tests performed on the Shroud of Turin (a historical piece of cloth that allegedly covered the body of Jesus when he was entombed). An R&D team used radiocarbon dating and other scientific tests to determine whether the stain was human blood as well as the age of both the cloth and stain. While the description of the process was intriguing, the teachers were informed that as a condition of the scientists being allowed to conduct their research, they had agreed not to reveal the results of the tests to the public (a possible religion/science conflict). No problem. Secrecy is a way of life at Los Alamos.

Back then, college students and their professors could take tours in the facility and listen to talks by the scientists. A favorite speaker was Fred Begay, the Navajo (Diné) physicist who offered an interpretation of nuclear science based on the complex metaphysics and the stories and cosmology he had learned growing up as an indigenous American. To those familiar with indigenous studies, his embrace of nuclear science may be reminiscent of the poet and storyteller Marilou Awiakta, who, in her book *Abiding Appalachia: Where Mountain and Atom Meet*, looks to Cherokee legend for foreknowledge of the atomic science conducted at Oak Ridge, Tennessee, once a part of the Cherokee homeland and now home to another national lab (see Killingsworth, *Facing It*, 112).

Bradbury Science Museum

Bradbury Science Museum

Since the LANL facilities are mainly closed to the public in these post-9/11 days, the story of Los Alamos is delivered to tourists of Nuclear New Mexico at the Bradbury Science Museum, sponsored and maintained by LANL, and the more modest Los Alamos Historical Museum. Both museums are located in the town of Los Alamos rather than on the LANL campus.

The Bradbury may well be hopping on the day of your tour. Even at midmorning on a Friday, you could arrive in the parking lot alongside a couple of vans, one loaded with school kids, the other with elderly folks (possibly denizens of a retirement facility). There will be others as well, many of them of that certain age, baby boomers who grew up in the shadow of the mushroom cloud.

As you walk in the door, the docent greeting visitors (on this day a young Hispanic man) tells everyone the schedule for films about the history of the lab and its mission. "The theater," he says, "is to your right. To your left are the models of Fat Man and Little Boy, the weapons that ended World War II." The weapons that *ended war*, he says, instead of the weapons that *made war* like never before and set a new standard for future weapons of mass destruction. The opening directions set the tone. The whole place seems oriented to *justification*.

Justification is a reflex rhetoric for scientists, project managers, and technical communicators these days. Their work lives and dies by The Grant. Without funding, there is no science. So the sell, the pitch, the justification are nearly as much a part of the work as the theory, the experiment, the application. Grantsmanship is wedded to the scientific method in the modern economy. Most federal grants (National Science Foundation funding, for example) require that some portion of project funding be devoted to "public education," so it's easy to imagine that at Los Alamos National Laboratory, a decent percentage of these appropriations are funneled into this museum. It is bright and shiny, well staffed, and densely informative.

"Securing the nation's defense" is forthrightly the number-one justification for the national lab, according to a central exhibit, and number one on all the lists in the displays outlining the purposes of research at Los Alamos. Other activities appear as sidelines: power production, computation, even environmental concerns. Power production research, you are instructed, has to do with streamlining and improving the delivery of nuclear power for peacetime uses, especially electricity. The researchers continue to chase the ever-receding promise of perpetually clean, safe, and affordable nuclear power plants. "There is a joke among fusion scientists," writes Kenneth Ford in his memoir on Los Alamos, "that fusion power is a decade away and always will be" (*Building the H Bomb*, 58n). Computational work focuses on computer modeling of explosions, which have been forbidden as underground tests since the 1992 test-ban treaty. Environmental research at Los Alamos builds on lessons learned from the cleanup of the "Cold War legacy" of radiation that still threatens the lab's grounds and surrounding lands.

Many different kinds of science are on display here, but you can see straight to the heart of the justification. Without research into nuclear weaponry and the history of the Atomic City as a fantasy world built by the scientific and military imagination, there would be no science done at Los Alamos. The research would return to the universities, and this place would become another stop on the tourist map of beautiful scenery—the blue skies, sheer cliffs, and pine forests of the southwestern mountains—perhaps distinguished by a monument or two extolling its exalted position in the history of research science and global warfare.

The exalted history prevails in the museum. Illustrated time lines structure the majority of the exhibits. They are busy with images—old news headlines, photographs of key players and scenes of battles and explosions, line drawings of engineering designs, artifacts of technology. The time lines are dense with text: explanations, narratives, factoids in paragraph form. The density of the information leaves the typical museum goer mildly stunned. You stare at an exhibit or two, read a few lines, and move to the next display—a wandering sampler of facts, stories, and rationales.

If you try to spend some time and really make an effort to absorb the explanations, you may be disappointed. An exhibit on the cleanup of the contamination around Los Alamos, for example, seems to say, "The best science available is being applied to this task as a model for similar tasks around the world"—and then say it again in different wording. And then again. You never move from general to specific, from theory to application; you just kind of stay in the middle range of meaning, where the sentences drone away and never develop. Like the cleanup task itself—with all those eternally radiating elements in the mix—the reading seems to have no end point, no ultimate lesson. It seems to say, "Move on, reader; this task could prove overwhelming." (As it turns out, the cleanup exhibit was removed not long after this writing, when the contamination became a live issue again, as activists from Amigos Bravos and other environmental watchdog groups brought it all back to the public's attention.)

Some of the exhibits are mildly interactive, not unlike the influential Exploratorium, the children's science museum in San Francisco founded by Frank Oppenheimer, Robert's brother, who became a science teacher after he lost his university job in the Red Scare of the 1950s. In one exhibit, a dark chunk of glassy rock is laid alongside another and the viewer is asked, which is human made and which is natural? If you can't tell, you lift the lid on the answer box and take a peek: the one on the left is the volcanic glass, obsidian; the one on the right is an artificially compressed hunk of formerly radioactive earth, now safe and indistinguishable from one of Mother Nature's rocks. The point is . . . what? That the things we make from the mess are as homey and enduringly charming as old Nature herself? Another possibility looms: that we have appropriated the power of the volcano that creates the glassy rock. We are the volcano, the potential disaster, with the power to rain fire and molten rock down on the heads of hapless villagers. Hominess departs; anxiety refuels.

Before leaving the museum, you can take the time to calculate your own personal radiation exposure using an interactive exhibit in which you respond to such questions as your age, the number of air flights you take per year, and the geographic location, altitude, and material construction of your home—mostly determining what the bomb scientists call "background radiation." Scientists' knowledge of cell biology and the biological effects of radioactive substances is enough to determine a link between millirems of exposure and life expectancy. Notice that there are no questions about how close you live to uranium mine tailings, a nuclear power plant, or nuclear waste-storage facility; whether you may have used Fiestaware or other irradiated dishes popular in the 1950s, and for how long; or whether you live downriver or downwind from a site that has had a leak in the past, such as Three Mile Island and Church Rock in 1979, Chernobyl in 1986, and Fukushima in 2011. (See Rogers, "Nuclear Power Plant Accidents," for a more extensive list of incidents since 1952.) For what it's worth, finish the calculation and drive on.

Los Alamos Historical Museum
One block west of the Bradbury stand the buildings once devoted to the Los Alamos Ranch School, which was commandeered by the

Fuller Lodge at the Los Alamos Ranch School

Manhattan Project, the faculty and students (dressed like Boy Scouts) sent packing. One young student, Sterling Colgate, later a Los Alamos physicist himself and (like Kenneth Ford) president of New Mexico Tech in Socorro, recalls a visit from a certain Mr. Smith and Mr. Jones to survey the property (see Else, *Day after Trinity*). The students saw through the dissembling—recognized Oppenheimer and Ernest Lawrence from pictures in their physics books—but found out only later what was up and how big it was. Statues of the main players, Oppenheimer and Groves, correctly identified and fully clothed in their historical significance, now stand in front of Fuller Lodge, once the main hall of the school. Fuller Lodge, which houses the town's art center and is available for rental by the public for conferences and other events, is a grand structure built of massive ponderosa pine logs, whose living cousins tower over the historical district of current Los Alamos.

Tucked in behind the lodge is the Los Alamos Historical Museum, which occupies the former guesthouse of the Ranch School. In scale and impressiveness, it forms a considerable contrast to the Bradbury Museum. The rooms are cramped and stuffed with displays, a little worse for the wear. Much of the history given in the Bradbury is recounted here but with less glitz, more dust, and more emphasis on what you might call the domestic side of the Atomic City. It shows how the uprooted scientists and their families lived in the equivalent of a military outpost, even as it celebrates their accomplishments.

Some of the numbers that key the displays to their explanations have fallen off the wall, and there are other signs of meager funding. But all that is about to change, according to the one docent assigned to guide visitors through the museum, a white-haired retired man who volunteers his time. Soon the museum and the surrounding remnant of the Ranch School will become part of the Manhattan Project National Historical Park. By the time you make your visit, everything will have changed—again.

As of this writing, the houses of the famous Bathtub Row behind the museum are still privately owned. Bathtub Row, now the official name on the street sign, was the nickname the scientists gave Twentieth Street during the project. The houses there, reserved for senior personnel with families, had bathtubs, unlike the barracks where single folks were housed with their down-the-hall showers. Iron was rationed, so new bathtubs were a rarity in war years. Oppenheimer's Bathtub Row house, at the end of the avenue on the corner with Peach Street, is slated to become a National Historic Landmark. It will emerge from the high shrubs and fences and open its doors to pilgrims seeking the presence of the great man.

Bathtub Row

The walk around Bathtub Row and back up Nineteenth Street leads to a couple of other historical structures worthy of note. Just as the tall pines recall the logs used to build the Fuller Lodge, the stones used in the construction of the houses on Bathtub Row recall the masonry of the "ancestral pueblo," partially excavated and reconstructed on the edge of the school's grounds. Also preserved is the school's fire station, no more than a pump house really, built of stones taken from the archaeological site, as the signage doesn't mind admitting. The stones are volcanic in origin, like much of the rock on this plateau. Like the bark of the pines, they are reddish in color. You may perceive a strange fit in this place, among the homes of the great ones, the grandness of the natural world, and the ancient drive of humanity to rearrange the things of the earth to suit the purposes of a long history. Don't be surprised if the walk returns you to the entrance of the historical museum in a pensive mood.

Leave the museum and look around Los Alamos, if you can bear it. It's an ordinary middle class–looking town, almost totally lacking

Pump house on the left, archaeological ruins in the foreground

in the southwestern charm of other towns in northern New Mexico with their adobe abodes and quaint mission churches. Los Alamos seems to have been transported out of the Midwest or lifted from the set for *Father Knows Best*, from Elm Street USA, and deposited for the life of science on the Pajarito Plateau in this remote region of the Southwest. The idea was to make the research scientists and their families comfortable (see Hunner, "Reinventing Los Alamos"), but the experience for an outsider is strange. It recalls the story "Mars Is Heaven!" from Ray Bradbury's *Martian Chronicles*. Earthmen arrive on Mars to find the homes of their memories restored and their dead friends and relatives alive in a world reconstructed by an alien race with less-than-welcoming motives.

Remnants of the Black Hole Surplus Store

Look closely and you might detect the barrack-like quality of World War II architecture still perceptible in some of the buildings. The history of the place is written in the very street names, you realize, as you navigate the intersection of Oppenheimer Drive and Trinity Drive.

But historical preservation has its limits in Los Alamos. Some of the memories are allowed to fade. The docent at the historical museum bemoans the loss of the old Mesa Library, for example, pointing to the shiny new library gleaming to the west of the walking tour. No doubt other changes are in store, for better and worse, with the coming of the Manhattan Project National Historical Park, which the docent welcomes as a chance for "us baby boomers" to do a better job at historical preservation. For now, the ruins of the Cold War often seem to recede from view.

Black Hole Surplus

Until 2012, you could have found a captivating preserve of Atomic Age artifacts over on Arkansas Street, a deposit of junk that formed a kind of alter ego to the neat houses on Bathtub Row and the gleaming exhibits of the Bradbury Museum. Black Hole Surplus was a curiosity not to be missed. It was operated by Ed Grothus, known as Atomic Ed. He called his store the Black Hole because "everything goes in but nothing comes out." By "everything" he meant the discarded hardware and sophisticated refuse of Los Alamos: "from oscilloscopes and galvanometers to Geiger counters and centrifuges—stacked in canyons in the Black Hole" (Memmott, "Los Alamos Landmark"). Atomic Ed once worked at Los Alamos but left the lab in 1969 in protest against the Vietnam War and was thereafter known locally as a peacenik and antinuclear advocate. By some estimates, he sold about 1 percent of the stuff he collected; the remainder piled up in silent testimony to . . . something. Grothus died in 2009, followed by his wife in 2012, at which point his descendants began to look for buyers for the stuff in the Black Hole, apparently with little success. As of this writing, the website for the Black Hole is still up (http://www.blackholesurplus.com/index.html), and the old place remains standing, with huge dumpster-like containers lining the yard behind the building, apparently full of unsellable surplus. The glass of the front window is still adorned with its sun-faded peace posters, and the parking lot sports a few items of interest, such as a metal daisy composed of propellers or airplane fuel tanks, perhaps the noses of small rockets. On top of the building stands a model of a molecule made mainly of bowling balls. Dust, rust, and economic necessity threaten the memories held within the Black Hole, memories that places like the Bradbury Museum and the proponents of nuclear tourism seek to shape anew.

Almost next door to the Black Hole stands a chapel dedicated to the cause of peace that old Atomic Ed pursued in his own style. It's an A-frame building in need of a new coat of paint. In front stands a matched pair of broken missiles (donated by the Black Hole?) that suggest the broken arrows signifying peace in the lore of the Old West. There's a plaque with this legend:

> "Remember your humanity, and forget the rest."
> In memory of Sir Joseph Rotblat (1908–2005)
> He left Los Alamos in December 1944 for conscience's sake and was awarded the Nobel Peace Prize in 1995 for decades of nuclear disarmament leadership. May many others follow his example.

Time your visit appropriately if you can, or be prepared to get caught up in the impatient rush away from the Atomic City. Not everyone who works at the lab lives in Los Alamos; some commute from Santa Fe and others from the towns and villages of the Española Valley, so that the roads around the town are filled with scurrying traffic at the end of the work shifts.

Why the rush? Historians and social commentators will tell you that not every resident of northern New Mexico swells with patriotic pride at the mention of Los Alamos. Besides the antinuclear folks, many of the local Hispanics and poorer families of various ethnicities harbor long-term resentments. The Los Alamos Ranch School

In memory of Sir Joseph Rotblat (1908–2005)

was not the only land confiscated, and small landholders were often compensated at a much lower rate than the big ranchers. The Ranch School and the local Anchor Ranch, for example, were awarded $250 per acre, while in other cases, payments ranged from $7 to $40 per acre. Many years later, a consolidated lawsuit known as the Pajarito Plateau Homesteaders Class Action was able, with the support of the New Mexico congressional delegation, to secure $10 million to be distributed to families unjustly compensated (Joseph Caldwell, pers. comm.). So US citizens have continued to pay for the Manhattan Project (and not just the national historical park) over the years, both in taxes and in unabated resentment.

Bandelier National Monument

Future archaeologists (perhaps from another world) may well puzzle over the junk heaps and radioactive garbage secreted around Los Alamos. The beings from the future will discover that the ruins of the Cold War, now rudely evident through the patina of middle-class comfort, are part of a deeper history everywhere evident on the Pajarito Plateau. The same day you visit the Atomic City, you can take a walk in one of several archaeological sites associated with the Bandelier National Monument, which shares space on the plateau with the National Lab. Again there appears the striking quality of Nuclear New Mexico, the natural beauty cozying up to the scientific and historical significance of each site, seemingly in contrast, but then surprisingly in cahoots. This time it's the stunning cliffs carved from volcanic tuff deposited centuries ago by the great explosion that produced the Valles Caldera a little south and west of Los Alamos, now a pastoral green valley lined with stands of aspen and spruce on steep slopes, where herds of elk graze and a great peaceful silence prevails year round.

Bandelier is not only a natural site of sublime beauty, but a national monument. As the Bradbury Museum tells the story of modern hu-

Archaeological site at Bandelier National Monument

manity on this lovely plateau, Bandelier tells the story of the natural history and ancient humanity. It is a story of continuous change, slow and steady like evolution, punctuated by cataclysmic events that accelerate the change—also like evolution, as it is understood in the theory of "punctuated equilibrium."

In Frijoles Canyon, where the main exhibits tell the story, you learn how the tuff from the volcano is layered over centuries of sandstone cut by streams, which are fed by springs and snowmelt from the Jemez Mountains. You read politely and curiously, but after a day in Los Alamos, you may find yourself tired of history and science and in a mood to get outdoors into the balm of sunshine and natural beauty. You leave the dioramas and explanatory placards in the visitor center and find the paved and numbered footpath that leads to a self-guided tour through the featured portion of the site, where the impressive cliff dwellings gradually appear among the irregular holes and crevasses in the yellow-orange rock of the high bluffs to your right. In the valley, you pass through a partial reconstruction of a city of ancient inhabitants whose history is lost. It is still a ruin, but call it an *enhanced* ruin. Just as the story has its unsolved mysteries—why the people left, for example: famine, flood, enemy attacks, witchery?—the preserved ancient village retains its ruin-like qualities, mirroring the gaps in historical knowledge. The round sunken kiva, where the ancient ones must have gathered ceremonially, remains roofless on the paved path between cliffs and creek, forever open to the elements and the peering eyes of archaeotourists and ecotourists. The same goes for the warren of small apartments around the path—maybe storage bins, maybe dwellings, maybe both—whose walls are reconstructed up to a few feet to give a sense of the size and arrangement, but left roofless and open.

The footpath leads you up to the cliff dwellings. Again, they are partially reconstructed. Crude but strongly constructed wooden ladders, on the model of those currently used in living pueblos, are provided so you can climb up and take photographs of yourself and your companions, who are probably too tall to be comfortable in the cells

(*overleaf*)
Footpath and ladder at Bandelier National Monument

abandoned by ancient humanity and can only look comic in this context. Poke your head out and smile for the camera.

Gaze down on the valley to the shapes of the former village outlined by the work of the archaeologists. Imagine the place teeming with the people of former times, now transformed into tourists clad in REI and Eddie Bauer gear, carrying not firewood and pots of water and bundles of corn and game, but cameras and binoculars.

Use those binoculars to spot the colorful birds in the trees and bushes, the black-headed grosbeak with its melodious trilling, the red face and bright yellow plumage of the western tanager, the sleek hawks among the taller trees, the occasional peregrine falcon on the cliffs, all drawn by the usually dependable water in the shady creek and the lush foliage for cover. Mule deer are plentiful as well and can sometimes be seen with their fawns near the shady creek. The tufted-eared Abert's squirrels (unique to the region) scold from the treetops and hurtle across the walkways. You might meet a black bear if you wander away from the paved paths and high-use areas.

Return your attention to the cliffs to take in the petroglyphs and a single colorful rock painting covered with glass to protect it from the elements. Some petroglyphs are abstract designs, spirals and the kinds of zigzag decorations you see on pottery. Others depict animals and people, giant gods and imagined beasts. The graffiti and art of the ancient villagers adds density to their story and connects them to other peoples across the Southwest, who used similar styles and symbols. If you peer up into some of the many crevasses, you may see bats hanging upside down—Mexican freetails or any of a dozen other species that reside in the monument.

The path eventually winds down among the cottonwoods and willows and crosses the creek. In warm weather, you can have a picnic in the shade with the sound of running water in your ears. As you munch your sandwich, muse on the disasters that have occasionally ravaged the place. As geologists often say, the present is the key to the past. In recent decades, drought has led to fire, the damage from which facilitates flooding along Frijoles Creek. The picnic area has

Archaeotourists in
the cliff dwellings

been destroyed, modified, and rebuilt more than once. Sixty percent of the park was burned by the Las Conchas Fire of 2011, leading to the closing of many areas, most of which are reopened as of this writing, though fire and flood continue to be a constant threat in this canyon. The same forces of nature may have driven out the ancient ones.

The hardy adventurer will find longer trails and further wonders. You can walk up the mesa opposite the cliff dwellings along gentle switchbacks and take the higher view of the valley. You'll need to keep going and cross another canyon to see the famous stone lions, a pair of elongated rocks with roughly hewn heads, tails, and folded legs, believed to be a shrine to the sleek predators carved by the original inhabitants of the area. Turning back to the visitor center at this point

Frijoles Creek
in winter

makes a thirteen-mile round trip (assuming you've followed the rudiments of the old trail and the remains of signage, which suffered heavy damage from the fire). If you press on (defying the seeming warning of the lions) to seek farther canyons and more evidence of early human traffic, you'll eventually come to the Painted Cave, more elaborately decorated with pictographs than any other place in the park, accessible only by an overnight hike for most people (a twenty-two-mile round trip up and down several canyons). These places remain shrines for some of the state's indigenous peoples, and the Park Service seems to have respected the sacredness of the lions and the cave by keeping access limited. Fire has made the trek more difficult yet.

Caution: As is true throughout mountainous New Mexico, the weather here can be unpredictable. After a 1978 trek past the stone lions, one of your guides woke up in a canyon campsite to over a foot of snow on the ground, yet still managed to hike to and from the Painted Cave for a second night's stay, and then back up and down the canyons for the return trip, in spite of nasty blisters immune to moleskin.

Even if you stay close to the easy walking on the paved path of the site proper, you won't be disappointed in your visit to Bandelier. But don't get so satisfied that you're tempted to skip the newest addition to the national monument, the Tsankawi site, the trailhead for which lies on the road leading back to Santa Fe. If you came here in days past, you might have explored this portion of the tour on your own, without benefit of signage and restrooms. You might have climbed up to the main site, perhaps an ancient hunting camp atop the low mesa, via footholds carved into the relatively gentle slope of the north side. In those days, you could find wild bees humming in rockbound hives with honey dripping from the openings, or catch sight of a gray fox slipping out of view as you approached, the very image of wariness.

Follow the trails provided by the Park Service to patrol the Tsankawi ruins, which have been left largely as they were found, without the reconstructions of old cliff dwellings, village squares, and ceremonial

Tsankawi Trail

kivas found in the main exhibits of Bandelier proper. Scouting for pottery shards and other signs left by the hunters, you may come upon a knapped piece of sharp black stone, then another and another. Hikers often leave little piles of the objects, the removal of which is illegal. Slowly you realize, deeply, that the ancient ones sat here on this mesa with its petroglyphs of game animals and hunter figures, mystical symbols and feathered gods. The hunters gazed across the shallow valley below to see deer, turkey, and elk passing by (all depicted here in stony memory) while patiently chipping away at the sharp edges of black chunks of obsidian or gray flint, carving a spearpoint or arrowhead to send into the shoulders and hearts of the meat animals or perhaps a human enemy.

Petroglyphs

Los Alamos National Laboratory
in the distance, viewed from
Tsankawi Trail

Then you realize that you're standing in a weapons factory. Looking westward, you see the chimneys and watchtowers and factory buildings of Los Alamos rising above the tree line on the plateau. The continuity between ancient and modern seems uncanny. Is war a natural state for humanity? Is Destroyer of Worlds a fated role in the long dream of humankind on earth?

The spearpoint and the atomic bomb: only the difference in scale trumps the strange similarity. But, as ecologists teach, scale cannot be underestimated. The spearpoint kills once or twice, at close range, and eventually dissolves into glassy sand; the bomb expands killing power to the far horizon, makes a new kind of glass, and leaves behind a radioactivity that virtually never dies.

Time, space, scale, humanity and its universe: everything has changed.

Albuquerque

An hour and a half south of Los Alamos is Albuquerque, the longtime population center of the state, which, though still a small city by today's standards, is the one true urban environment in the Land of Enchantment. In the national mind, its urban status is cinched by recent television crime shows, like the witness-protection drama *In Plain Sight* and the hugely popular saga of a chemistry teacher turned methamphetamine merchant, *Breaking Bad*. (If you're so inclined, you can book the Breaking Bad Tour in Albuquerque and visit some of the key settings for the show.) In the world of television and pulp fiction, urbanization appears to be measured by the variety and intensity of a town's criminal life, with New York and Los Angeles setting the standard. That doesn't mean that the town in question is truly unsafe for the casual tourist or the well-protected resident. At best, urbanization as measured by criminal presence is a metaphor; at worst, it's a mere impression that may or may not be supported by statistics and everyday experience. And crime isn't the only element in the mix. New Orleans got on the map early because of its culture and exoticism.

Part of Albuquerque's appeal as a destination of cultural fantasy and touristic interest, beyond its southwestern charm mingled with its urban amenities and recent notoriety in TV drama, is the history it shares with Los Alamos and Carlsbad on the map of Nuclear New Mexico. The city banks on this history. The local minor-league baseball team, to take one example, was once known as the Dukes, a rather old-fashioned reference to the nickname of Duke City, which commemorates the Spanish Duke of Alburquerque (as the name of the original Spanish town was spelled), who gave the New World settlement his name. But now the AAA affiliate of the Colorado Rockies enjoys a shinier, more modern and scientific moniker that invokes the city's nuclear heritage: the Isotopes.

Kirtland Air Force Base / Sandia National Laboratories

When Los Alamos emerged as the home of the Manhattan Project, with a secret office in Santa Fe, the military arm of the operation needed a transportation and communication hub. Kirtland Air Force Base in Albuquerque fit the bill.

In 1939, the Army Air Corps purchased Oxnard Field on the mesa west of Albuquerque (which began as a private facility) and completed construction of a new air base. Named Kirtland Army Airfield in 1941, it soon became an instrumental training ground for pilots as well as combat and engineering crews, including those who flew the B-29 that dropped Fat Man and Little Boy on Japan. By 1946, training activities ceased as the facility's purpose was shifted to ballistic weapons delivery systems, testing of which was conducted on a nearby base in the Manzano Mountains. Renamed Kirtland Air Force Base (AFB) in 1947, the base soon housed the Special Weapons Command (renamed the Air Force Special Weapons Center in 1952). In 1971 Kirtland merged with two other area air bases, Sandia

Sign near entrance to Kirtland Air Force Base

Albuquerque from
Sandia Crest

and Manzano. According to its website, "the [current] mission of the [Kirtland AFB's] 377th Air Base Wing is to execute nuclear, readiness, and support operations for American air power." The facility is "a center for research, development and testing of non-conventional weapons, space and missile technology, laser warfare and much more" ("Kirtland Air Force Base Welcome").

Of course, like many government institutions engaged in ongoing nuclear research, Kirtland is not a tourist destination. Nothing to see here, pilgrim, although perhaps you can stand at the fence and take comfort and pride in knowing that the US government is active in both national defense and "space technology."

Associated with the air base is another national laboratory. Established in 1945 as "the ordnance design, testing, and assembly arm of Los Alamos National Laboratory," and named in 1948 for the strikingly crested mountains just east of Albuquerque, Sandia National Laboratories was created by the US government as another center for research and development of nuclear weaponry. Designated a Department of Energy national laboratory in 1979, it is currently managed by "National Technology and Engineering Solutions of Sandia, LLC, a wholly owned subsidiary of Honeywell International, Inc." Its mission includes the following points:

- anticipating and resolving emerging national security challenges
- innovating and discovering new technologies to strengthen the nation's technological superiority
- creating value through products and services that solve important national security challenges
- informing the national debate where technology policy is critical to preserving security and freedom throughout our world ("Sandia National Laboratories: Mission").

If you grew up in New Mexico, you may have heard rumors about a secret facility dug into the Manzano Mountains, the small range just south of the Sandias in the long line of peaks and mesas that form the eastern edge of the Rio Grande Valley. Reminiscent of a James Bond movie or the many cavernous steel-and-concrete bunkers that you see in science fiction cinema, the massive cave near Albuquerque was supposed to have provided storage for weapons associated with the work of the national labs, notably the assembly projects that went on at Sandia Labs.

The rumors turn out to be true, according to Ian Bogost, the author of a stylish (if esoteric) book called *Alien Phenomenology, or What It's Like to Be a Thing*. Among other things, Bogost reflects on changes in human consciousness (or the lack of changes) resulting from the transformation of our world, including changes initiated by atomic technology. His very first page muses on this extraordinary fact: "In the hollowed-out Manzano Mountain, the US Armed Forces Special Weapons Command once stashed the nation's largest domestic nuclear weapons repository, some 2,450 warheads as of the turn of the millennium." It was a mountain full of bombs, with barely imaginable explosive power.

4. The museum replaced the old National Atomic Museum in downtown Albuquerque. In the New Mexico chapters of *A Nuclear Family Vacation: Travels in the World of Atomic Weaponry*, Nathan Hodge and Sharon Weinberger describe the old museum as quaintly unimpressive, something like the way we found the Los Alamos Historical Museum. Before 9/11, it was located on the grounds of Kirtland Air Force Base, and then it was moved downtown and finally to Eubanks Avenue with its new name. The new museum, which opened after Hodge and Weinberger's book went to press, is more impressive even than the Bradbury in Los Alamos. Hodge and Weinberger were most interested in the weapons displays at the old museum. They had found nothing at Trinity Site to spark their imaginations but, as defense reporters, eagerly covered the scandals and administrative problems associated with Los Alamos National Lab over the years. Different nuclear tourists take away different impressions of an always-changing historical landscape.

The repository, or what's left of it, is like the WIPP site proper, the working buildings of the national labs, the military bases, and other secret and protected facilities in the state: you can't go there. The closest you can get—other than flying over in a commercial jet destined for the cheerful "Sunport," Albuquerque's international airport, which once shared space with the warplanes and airfields of Kirtland but is now separated by a few city blocks—is the National Museum of Nuclear Science and History, at the foot of the Sandias on Eubank Avenue.[4]

National Museum of Nuclear Science and History

On entering the structure, the chrome and glass lit by the bright sun suggest that you've found another museum that resists the dusty gloom usually associated with places that preserve the past. Here is a museum of enlightenment, celebrating the bright beam of progress, of science and technology, of flights to the sun on wings of polished chrome rather than the waxed feathers of Icarus—the very Sunport of atomic history.

You cross a floor tiled with the periodic chart of the elements. Your thoughts may scurry back to chemistry class, the mysterious letters and numbers arranged in columns and rows above the blackboard at the front of the lecture hall, the teacher pointing to show the square devoted to helium from the balloon, oxygen from the air and water, hydrogen from the water and the bomb, lead with its Latin abbreviation (Pb), the noble gases lying inert on the right side of the chart. Now your feet move over the same squares and symbols, with special colors to highlight the new elements of nuclear science at the bottom of the chart, the atoms with the largest atomic weights, which nature never produced without the promptings of science—the likes of einsteinium, atomic number 99, created in 1952 by the blast of the first H-bomb tested (the one named Mike) in the Pacific Ocean. The new element was named for the man who by that time was mortified by the history of the bomb, though he had famously urged President Roosevelt to pursue its production. Some of those present at the test wanted to name the element pandemo- nium, but Einstein got the dubious honor and was allotted his square on the periodic table (McPhee, *Curve of Binding Energy*, 83).

By the time you look up from the tiles of the chart, you've arrived at a pictorial time line that tells the story of how scientists, including Einstein, unlocked the secrets of the atom. You may linger over the story of Werner Heisenberg, famous for his Uncertainty Principle, a key contributor to quantum mechanics, and a German citizen who directed the Nazi efforts to build an atomic weapon. Heisenberg ultimately declared the bomb impossible and at first, in his prison cell in France after the defeat of Germany, refused to believe the news that the Allies had succeeded in exploding not one, but two bombs over Japanese cities (Monk, *Robert Oppenheimer*, 468–69). One of the museum's docents is fond of the theory that Heisenberg didn't actually fail but sabotaged the German version of the Manhattan Project, either out of camaraderie with his fellow physicists on the Allied side or worry over the consequences of bequeathing the bomb to future generations. You want to forgive your scientific heroes—along with such philosophical brethren as Martin Heidegger—for joining the Nazi cause. How could great thinkers have accepted Hitler as their leader and countenanced the actions of the Nazis, much less participated in the program? A German philosopher of the preceding generation, old Nietzsche, had an answer to the question: *human, all too human*. Let the light shine on the human failures of the past, both in science and in judgment.

It turns out that this introductory time line, as a mode of presenting information, is the exception rather than the rule at the museum. The Albuquerque facility mostly avoids the overloaded time lines that dominate the Bradbury Museum in Los Alamos. Even the history-of-

The National Museum of Nuclear Science and History

physics display is less wordy, with fewer technical diagrams and long explanations, focusing more on people and photographs of the old scientists with their crazy hair and funny mustaches. Here the information is far less dense and off-putting than the same information at the Bradbury. It is, as the computer people say, more user-friendly. Instead of turning you away, puzzled by the mysteries of science, the displays invite you in.

Bearing to the right as you pass the time line, you enter the stream of history. You stroll through time, with more artifacts and models and fewer display boards crammed with text. You may pass quickly by things you've seen at Los Alamos, the stories of atrocities like the Bataan Death March and the Nazi camps, stories that explain the feelings people on the Allied side had toward the enemy; the story of the Manhattan Project with photos of Oppenheimer (looking like Bob Dylan in one youthful pose), Lawrence, Groves, Teller, and others; the pictures of wartime Los Alamos and the Trinity experiment; the models of "the gadget," the first bombs, the airplanes involved; the black-and-white photographs of destruction in the Japanese cities.

Next comes the aftermath of the war. Pause for a moment over the Civil Defense display. Watch the duck-and-cover drill explained in a film for elementary school students, complete with advice from older kids about what to do when you see the flash (duck under your desk and cover your head), the scariness deflected by the film's cartoon mascot, Bert the Turtle (make like a turtle and draw into your shell at the first sign of danger). The film runs in an endless loop, stuck in the moment of time, on a vintage black-and-white TV, the screen impossibly small by today's standards. The TV sits on a low table inside a life-sized model of a home fallout shelter, cross-sectioned for viewing on the tour through time. The furnishings include bare concrete-block walls, an army cot for sleeping, ten-gallon water storage cans, packaged foods (both vintage brands and something like civilian C rations, including "Survival Biscuits" with the Civil Defense logo on the side), even a Civil Defense "Sanitation Kit" (no explanation of how to use it).

The downhill ramp by the bomb shelter urges you forward into a large room with models and photos, text cards and film clips featuring "delivery systems"—weapons, that is. The room is crammed with embodiments of the nuclear threat, from tactical battlefield weapons (which tried to solve the problem of how to destroy the charging infantry of the enemy without blowing yourself up or irradiating your own comrades with the same blast) to missiles with thermonuclear warheads for long-distance damage. The muscle behind the Cold War doctrine of Mutual Assured Destruction and tentative world peace built on the principle of Détente (the idea that if you have enough of the right weapons, the enemy won't dare start something) stands here before your eyes.

Besides the user-friendliness of the displays (frightful though they are), another thing that makes the Albuquerque museum different from its counterpart in Los Alamos is that it soft-pedals the justifications and rationalizations for the development of the bomb. In fact, some effort is made to achieve a kind of journalistic balance in the story. There are small displays about Japanese survivors from Nagasaki and Hiroshima, for example, and a lurid red-lighted section on civil defense in the Soviet Union—the other side of the story. The former enemy is humanized rather than demonized.

When justification does play a part, it's far subtler, almost subliminal. In the weapons room, for instance, take a close look at the small exhibit on the Ohio class of nuclear submarines, which have the capability to deliver thermonuclear death from beneath the oceans at various locations at any time. The subs roam the earth in constant motion—on alert, ready to strike—to this day. In the display, the absence of dates can be misleading. The first of the subs, the USS *Ohio*, was "launched April 7, 1979," ten years before the fall of the Berlin Wall. A list of the names of other *Ohio*-class subs is also provided, but no dates, obscuring the fact that, as Elaine Scarry makes clear in her book *Thermonuclear Monarchy*, most of these ships were launched well after the end of the Cold War and still roam the seas. The display, one of the last you encounter in the weapons room, sits directly across from a transitional exhibit depicting the fall of the Berlin Wall with the title "The Cold War Ends." From this display, you might conclude (wrongly) that weapons development and deployment ended with the fall of the Soviet Bloc. If you walk out of the room, you seem to leave it all behind. Rooms beyond this one, which focus on the present, deal with peacetime applications like medical technology (from X-rays to radiation therapy and modern imaging techniques) and nuclear power plants (both existing models and the improved but still unrealized versions). There's also a small exhibit on the WIPP site, with its insistent theme of safety and the care with which Cold War detritus is handled. Put up by the Department of Energy, the WIPP display replicates the Carlsbad presentations point for point. The depictions of both present and future nuclear power may leave you feeling safe and hopeful. But take care: as the crowded time lines of Los Alamos honestly depict, the story of weapons development continues after the end of the Cold War and spreads to other countries—beyond the superpowers of the era, the United States, Russia, and China—to include the United Kingdom, France, Israel, India, Pakistan, and now North Korea and who knows who else, with nuclear weapons threatening always to become available to freelancing terrorists in the form of a dirty bomb or suitcase-sized weapon.

The message that begins to emerge in Albuquerque resonates with the Carlsbad theme: it's all behind us now—don't worry, be happy. Buttressing the message is the aura of nostalgia, which you've felt all over the state. It's practically patriotic in New Mexico to indulge in fifties nostalgia. "Oldies" rock-and-roll bands—playing Little Richard, Fats Domino, and Buddy Holly songs—are often featured alongside mariachi and norteño bands at local fiestas (with many groups mixing the genres). From the preserved motor lodges with their vintage neon signs in Tucumcari and other stops along the historical Route 66 to the caverns at Carlsbad and the alien paraphernalia in Roswell, nostalgia for the 1950s signals the moment that New Mexico entered the mainstream American imagination. The state's association with the bomb, as much as anything else, precipitated the new image, and at the National Museum of Nuclear Science and History, nostalgia is cultivated with a quiet passion.

Its presence dominates the room devoted to Atomic Age culture, into which you proceed directly from the weapons room, passing the "Cold War Ends" exhibit along the way. Here you'll find an atomic-themed race car; an exhibit on the Boy Scouts of America (the Atomic Energy Merit Badge, inaugurated in 1963, then reconceived as the Nuclear Science Merit Badge in 2005, adorned with Einstein's famous equation $E = mc^2$); a display on the "protest and satire culture" of the 1960s, featuring images of Bob Dylan, Peter, Paul, and Mary, and Dr. Strangelove; even a sitting area with 1950s furniture, a retro yellow breakfast-room set with linoleum-and-chrome table and chairs ("Mom had one just like it!"), and a period couch with end tables and lamps. Here's a comfortable spot to take a break and watch TV, as in the den of a baby boomer's childhood home. The up-to-date, though rather small, television set is the one anachronism, along with the show that's running at the moment: the *Frontline* episode "Inside Japan's Nuclear Meltdown," about the 2011 Fukushima disaster, which collides with the prevailing trend toward nostalgic obliteration of the present.

Back in the culture room, you'll find that despite first impressions, the artifacts are far from randomly arranged. The word *room*, as applied here to the weapons and culture exhibitions, is used loosely. Really the space is more open, and probably flexible, with cubicle-like separators organizing the walk through time. The openness of the rooms and the ability to move in and out of the tour of atomic history may be designed to convey a feeling of freedom, informality, and relaxation in the museum goer. It also hints at the interconnected nature of history, the military, science, and the culture at large—all saturated with nuclear science and history.

The key to the arrangement in the culture room—and the underlying message—appears in the display of movie posters adorning the walls, which begins as you enter from the weapons room and continues clockwise around the exhibit. The posters are arranged in roughly four groups, corresponding to "the four periods of Atomic Culture." The theory of the four periods comes from a 2002 book with the provocative title *Atomic Culture: How We Learned to Stop Worrying and Love the Bomb*, edited by Scott C. Zeman and Michael A. Amundson.[5] The book focuses on popular culture and includes chapters on film, photography, community planning, comic books, iconography, and other topics. The most influential idea comes from the introduction: Zeman and Amundson's division of the postwar years into the four periods of Early, High, Late, and Post Atomic Culture.

As the museum placards explain, Early Atomic Culture, 1945–48, begins when the news of the bomb becomes public after the destruction of Hiroshima and Nagasaki and is marked by a mood that ranges from elation and national pride over the end of the war to puzzlement and fascination over the meaning of the new discoveries. High Atomic Culture, 1949–63, begins with the news that the Soviet Union has developed its own bomb and the onset of the Cold War and arms race, the mood colored by worries over destruction of the world and a combative, even aggressive attitude toward the other side. Late Atomic Culture, 1964–91, begins in the wake of the Cuban Missile Crisis and the Kennedy assassination and includes the Vietnam Era, when the mood shifts and people grow more critical of nuclear buildup and the government in general, when the "Cold War consensus" is said to collapse. Post Atomic Culture, from 1992 to the present, follows the end of the Cold War and presents a curious mix of nostalgia and confusion over what comes next.

The categories offer an interesting sense of movement through time and the evolution of atomic culture, from early schlock to sixties satire and on to the current nostalgia backgrounded with post-9/11 paranoia. Sample the shifting moods of the posters: Roy Rogers in *Bells of Coronado* (1949), in which the cowboy hero as insurance investigator uncovers a plot to sell uranium to a foreign power; Mickey Rooney's 1954 *The Atomic Kid*, featuring a goofy uranium prospector

5. The theory of periods is unacknowledged in the museum placards. Thanks to Professor Lee Ann Powell of Washington State University for helping with the identification of this source.

who gains special powers from eating an irradiated peanut butter sandwich and helps the FBI break up a spy ring; *On the Beach* (1959), the dark apocalypse of ordinary people living in Australia, waiting for the deadly fallout to spread during the last days of a world contaminated by nuclear war in the Northern Hemisphere; the 1964 Cold War crisis film *Fail Safe*; the 1966 spoof on mass hysteria *The Russians Are Coming, the Russians Are Coming*; the docudrama *Silkwood* (1983) about the death of Karen Silkwood, a worker concerned with safety violations in an Oklahoma plutonium processing plant; the 1995 crisis film *Crimson Tide*, which forthrightly considers the danger of nuclear submarines riding the high seas in the post–Cold War era; and the nostalgic portrayal of the Kennedy administration during the Cuban Missile Crisis, *Thirteen Days* (2000).

The theory of periods, you may notice, has its problems. You might question the distinction between Early and High Atomic Culture, or notice the subtler interchange of moods within High and Late Atomic Culture. Most troubling of all is the very idea of Post Atomic Culture, the period still underway. Are nostalgia and confusion all we have to show as a cultural response to the nuclearization of the world? "To be sure," says the museum placard devoted to Post Atomic Culture, "Americans are still concerned with nuclear weapons, especially in the hands of 'rogue nations' or terrorists, but the atom seems to have lost its cultural centrality." Say it's not true! The upswing of nuclear tourism suggests otherwise. And anyway, we've got a tour to run.

Warning: While contemplating the enormity of a human creation that has swallowed a nation's identity, permeated its culture, and generated its heroes for more than three generations, you might feel a momentary shortness of breath or sensation of vertigo. If so, a whiff of fresh southwestern air might prove salubrious.

Go back to the weapons room and take the alternate route out of the museum into the backyard of nuclear science and history, which contains artifacts too large to keep indoors. Before you look around, breathe deeply in the clear air; let the sun warm you.

Then survey the impressive junk of the Nuclear Age. Walk beneath

B-29 Superfortress
in the background

the wings of the B-29 Superfortress from World War II and gaze on the type of bomb port from which emerged the weapons innocuously named Fat Man (Nagasaki, August 9, 1945) and Little Boy (Hiroshima, August 6, 1945); then stroll along the sleeker form of the B-52, and the yet sleeker intercontinental ballistic missiles; and look upon the cruise missiles, the forerunners of the unmanned drones that race through the skies of today's nightmares.

Take a seat on the bench beneath the politely provided sun shade, placed in the improbable midst of retired weapons that could have destroyed the world—and ask yourself whether it's really only nostalgia and confusion that you feel. Don't shy away from the other moods and emotions—pride of accomplishment, nationalistic zeal, wonder in the face of the technological sublime, anger and fear (or arousal) at the scale and intensity of human aggression, even futility over a civilization whose greatest minds produced such destructive power and whose concretely imagined futures include death by gradual warming or instant incineration.

Entertain the feelings; they are your legacy, and you their rightful heir.

Sandia Peak

As far as natural beauty goes, the Albuquerque area is no different from other stops on the tour of Nuclear New Mexico. Visitors from the eastern and northwestern parts of the nation, or from the temperate zones such as the Europeans enjoy, often find the desert landscape an acquired taste. But most travelers are intrigued if not favorably impressed by the special beauty of the arid high plains across which the city sprawls. The American Southwest was first promoted as a tourist destination by the Santa Fe Railroad, whose stops in New Mexico on the way to the Grand Canyon and points west were hailed for the rugged and colorful landscape as well as the cultural diversity offered by the Native American homelands and the Spanish influences

Sandia Peak
Tram

in architecture and lifeways—places to buy pottery and jewelry, to listen to mariachis and watch colorful dances, to sample hot chili and marvel at adobe villages.[6] Then came the science fictional imagination, which was widely cultivated in the alien-seeming, unearthly landscapes of the Southwest (again from the perspective of the Anglo and European outlook that takes the temperate zone as the norm). If you ever heard anybody argue that the moon landings were faked, you probably know that Arizona and New Mexico are often named as the places where it all really happened, the cameras running as men in space suits moonwalked out in some remote desert. One way or the other, the novelty of the place rarely fails to leave some mark on people raised in lands shaped by frequent rainfall, moderate temperatures, deciduous forests, broad meadows, and wide lawns.

Albuquerque suggests the wide-open spaces of the American West—the vistas, the big skies, the far horizon. A retreat to the desert and the mountains may offer balm to the tourist beset by lingering feelings from the weapons room and garden of nuclear delivery systems at the museum. If it doesn't bring complete relief—the alien spaces may well be too strange and unsettling—then certainly a tour of the land may satisfy one desire arising from immersion in nostalgia and confusion over the condition of our nuked-out world—the need for *perspective, to take the long view, to rise above it all.* All these things you can do, if not figuratively, as we usually mean when we say such things—"I've been to the mountaintop!"—then literally, on the tram ride up to Sandia Peak. Or, for the hardier tourist, you can do it right and take the trail up the side of the rugged mountain, maintained by the Cibola National Forest. This land is your land, public land. So go to the mountaintop.

The tramway offers a few advantages. Besides ease of travel, it presents a lesson in fast-changing outlooks—an example of the shift in consciousness that all big technology brings, including the technology of nuclear war. Built some fifty years ago to transport skiers from Albuquerque up the rocky western cliffs and canyons of the mountain and over to the skiable slopes on the snowier, forested

6. Dr. Caroline Jean Fernald, director of the Millicent Rogers Museum in Taos, provided pertinent information on the influence of tourism on indigenous artifacts and lifeways in the Southwest.

eastern side, the tram provides a powerful shift of perspective, typical of technological options—a speeding up of time and a spreading out of space. In a mere fifteen minutes, you climb 3,500 feet from a starting point already well above the city proper, to which you have driven or perhaps bicycled on the fine trails and wide boulevards of the city's northeast heights. For the adult price of twenty dollars, you can board the Swiss-built car, swinging on its mighty cable, among some thirty other tourists, and begin an upward float.

To the south, the edges of the high Sandias come into view, then the Manzanos (where the cavern of warheads was hidden), until finally you can see all the way to Socorro, with the Magdalenas rising from the plains west of the brave river's brown ribbon, and to the east, the smaller Oscuras that border Trinity Site, and on a clear day the Sacramentos with their towering peak, Sierra Blanca. Looking due west as you rise, you may find the fast-shifting perspective hallucinatory. Notice the little cinder cones on the mesa west of Albuquerque, where a young Ed Abbey and some of his fellow pranksters once set a fire of old tires to summon the University of New Mexico geologists and fire department to check out the possibility of a live volcano close to the city (Cahalan, *Edward Abbey*, 63). The cones seem larger at the starting point at the end of Tramway Road and then grow smaller as you go up, until they disappear entirely into the brown stretch of land in that direction. Farther to the west rise the broad shoulders of Mount Taylor, nearly twelve thousand feet high, one of the four corners of the Navajo world. It grows larger, as if to guard the way to the city of Grants and the uranium fields on its far side, then smaller, taking its place in the panoply of peaks in every direction, emerging out of the high plains as you rise above it all on the strength of the cable.

The view to the north and east are blocked by Sandia Peak, but even in those directions, the perspective shifts to offer superhuman vision, like time-lapse photography, of the changes in ecosystems as you climb so much faster than even the best legs or a good mule could carry you. The piñon-juniper zone yields to the colder, higher canyons with their ponderosa pines and Douglas firs; the tree-sized yuc-

The Manzanos viewed from Sandia Crest

cas are demoted to the stunted brush of Spanish daggers; the bushy hills become craggy castles and steeples of bare rock, where even the prickly pear cactus struggles to find a foothold. Looking far below as the tram ascends, you might see the shadow of a big hawk that circles slowly above the tram. Look up, and you might see its red tail shining in the sunlight.

"What happens if the machine malfunctions?" Imagine the nerve of an old man asking such a thing of the tram's "conductor," a young fellow who takes questions and entertains the tram riders with his generationally bound humor that often misses the mark.

"You mean like rappelling down from here?" Everybody looks downward with an involuntary gulp. Ha ha.

"No. We just hang out and wait," he says. "There used to be an escape plan, but getting everybody into harnesses and dropping them down to the trails seemed a little risky and too slow anyway. No, it's better just to wait it out. Let the mechanics get it fixed."

You look around at the people in the car and wonder at the old guy's indiscretion at asking the question. "Hey, buddy," you may be thinking, "there're kids in here."

But then again, why not? Let us all face the prospect—stranded by our technology, our reaching for the top, our unending need to go faster and easier and higher, the need for transcendence, rising above our station, taking the view from the tower, the lord of the manor's view. Muse on the perils, worthy companions, young and old. They are many, and they are real. If nothing else, the thought will add to the thrill. Enjoy the adrenalin, children!

The doors open safely at the top, where you can stroll the trails on the crest, looking west toward the city and the desert beyond and east toward the forested ski slopes and hills and the famous Llano Estacado, the staked plains named by Coronado's expedition in search of the fantasized cities of gold, stretching to the horizon. The vista opens to the north as well, and you see the Jemez Mountains and place yourself in relation to Los Alamos.

In the summer, you can take a series of trails on some grand hikes along the crest and into the canyons. But in the winter, bring your skis, or take in the view and head back down to escape the high winds that accumulate in the canyons below and blast over the ridgetop. Even in the spring, the wind will be high, and the trails can be icy and treacherous. The tram conductor will tell you that careless tourists slip and fall to their death every year, not to mention the casualties among risk-taking rock climbers and boulder hoppers. "Respect the mountain," he says, "and we'll get along just fine."

The search for perspective will bring you to a series of little metal tubes, crude telescopes lined up on the banister of the wooden walkway along the ridgetop. The tubes point toward features in the western and southern vistas, the names printed on a sign alongside. They identify Mount Taylor, Los Lunas, Ladron Peak, the Magdalenas, Sierra Blanca, Capitan Peak, and other landmarks. But here's a surprise among the natural wonders: Kirtland Air Force Base and the National Museum of Nuclear Science and History. Even the Forest Service recognizes the centrality of Nuclear New Mexico among the natural points of interest.

Then something that the tram conductor said may come back to you. "You can see a hundred miles in every direction on a clear day," he says, "but it's all New Mexico. A lot of people think you can see our neighboring states of Texas, Arizona, and Colorado, and one guy was even convinced he could see back to his home state of Connecticut. But it's all New Mexico."

A hundred miles in every direction—the measurement, the perspective may give pause to the nuclear tourist. In an article on early experiments in civil defense conducted in the community of Los Alamos, the historian Jon Hunner says, "Precautions like quick evacuations from a target area and duck-and-cover drills might have helped in the case of an attack by an atomic bomb such as the one used against Hiroshima. But with the increased strength of hydrogen bombs, such measures were no longer effective. . . . Civil Defense was a response to a grim reality, but after the Soviets detonated their hydrogen bomb in November 1955, the drills acted more like a placebo, given to citizens in a target area to help them deal with their fears" ("Reinventing Los Alamos," 43). The kill zone of the radiation from a hydrogen bomb was deemed to stretch a hundred miles in every direction and persist for much longer than a person could reasonably hide in a home fallout shelter. A bomb dropped in Los Alamos would produce a kill zone that could reach the place you stand, here on Sandia Peak. One dropped on Kirtland Air Force Base could encompass the entire vista, depending on variables like wind speed. A grim reality indeed.

Looking north toward Los Alamos, you can identify the volcanic shape of the Valles Caldera, a massive explosion in its time, but with a visible and immediate kill zone limited to the flow of its lava and the flight of its boulders and ash.[7] Imagine instead a hydrogen bomb exploding in the same place, the fireball and mushroom cloud rising, the mountain obliterated like some small Pacific island, the blistering zone of death spreading as far as the eye can see from one of these tall peaks—and after that, the spread of the radiation.

Everything has changed.

7. We do not mean to underestimate the long-term effect of volcanic eruption, knowing that volcanic ash from any big explosion may affect worldwide climate as the ash travels around the world on the prevailing air currents. According to the National Center for Atmospheric Research (UCAR Center for Science Education), "Most of the particles spewed from volcanoes cool the planet by shading incoming solar radiation. The cooling effect can last for months to years depending on the characteristics of the eruption. Volcanoes have also caused global warming over millions of years during times in Earth's history when extreme amounts of volcanism occurred, releasing greenhouse gases into the atmosphere."

The Shadow Tour

Dark Legacies

If you tell most folks, even New Mexicans, that you are taking the tour of Nuclear New Mexico, they may well say, "You mean Trinity and Los Alamos—what else is there?" The action of the two best-known historical novels set in Nuclear New Mexico—Martin Cruz Smith's *Stallion Gate* and Joseph Kanon's *Los Alamos*—alternates between the site where the bomb was made and the site where it was first tested, with a few side trips to Santa Fe. The two novelists (both from out of state) vividly depict the local scenery and culture but leave the impression that nuclear history cut a deep road, like a modern Santa Fe Trail, between Los Alamos and Trinity Site and left the rest of the state to evolve in innocent wilderness, dotted by quaint villages and small-time agriculture, a mainly rural land still dealing with the slower changes of a colonial past and the old Industrial Revolution, the coming of the railroad and the automobile and the demand for coal, oil, and gas. Some well-informed guides, like Hodge and Weinberger in *A Nuclear Family Vacation*, may add Albuquerque to the Atomic Trail because of Sandia Labs. Even fewer will think of Carlsbad and the WIPP site, which strives for invisibility—with some success, it seems. Like the two novels, and the recent television series *Manhattan*, public memory seems to start and end with the Manhattan Project and attach to its key places, merging with Cold War nostalgia.

A slightly different story is told by the densely informative time lines of the Bradbury Museum in Los Alamos. These displays won't let you rest with the impression that the war is over, regardless of the bang at the end of World War II or the whimpering close of the

Sign on fence surrounding Trinity Site

Cold War. Wars press forward into the present. Hitler may have killed himself, the emperor of Japan may have finally relented and surrendered after thousands died instantly at Hiroshima and Nagasaki, and the USSR may have fallen, but now others have the bomb. The time lines show the tests by France, by China, by India and Pakistan. The process of enriching uranium, increasing the ratio of U-235 to U-238, and of producing plutonium is explained and illustrated, resonating with worries about what's going on in the power plants in Iran and other potential enemy nations. The ongoing crises with North Korea would come as no surprise to the authors of the Los Alamos time lines. Justification of a place like Los Alamos requires a measure of realism missing in the Department of Energy assurances at the WIPP site that the Cold War is over. It may be over, the Bradbury time lines say, but the Nuclear Age, now nearly a lifetime old, presses on, surely and relentlessly. The time lines are long and open ended.

The history of Nuclear New Mexico is also open ended. It continues to unfold not only in the work of the research labs and air bases but also in what activists, journalists, scholars, government officials, and health advocates call "legacy issues." The legacy problem in the Utah-Nevada landscape has to do with the fallout from bomb testing and its lingering effects on the bodies of downwinders. A similar set of issues informs complaints of Tularosa Basin residents in New Mexico, who allegedly suffer from a higher-than-normal incidence of cancer owing to the first test at Trinity Site. Environmental groups like Amigos Bravos likewise continue to track the progress of the cleanup around Los Alamos—a dark environmental legacy.

But in the Landscape of Enchantment, legacy issues are most often associated with accidents and exposure related primarily to uranium mining. Recent writers like Peter Eichstaedt, Valerie Kuletz, and Judy Pasternak have told the story of the uranium rush in the Four Corners region (where the state borders of Utah, Arizona, Colorado, and New Mexico come together), especially in the Navajo Nation, or Diné Bikéyah, to use the people's own name for their tribal lands, transliterated into English, instead of the more familiar name, which comes from the Spanish.[1] In Diné Bikéyah, the need for mining was sold to the Navajo (Diné) as an act of patriotism comparable to military service in the war as well as a source of much-needed income in the deep rural backcountry of this red-rock desert. Pasternak tells how the Navajo people were once considered practically immune to cancer, but now exhibit rates far higher than the national norm in places where the mining was most intense and the legacy remains especially active.

The longtime activist and former journalist Chris Shuey, now working for the Southwest Research and Information Center (SRIC) in Albuquerque, tells how over five hundred abandoned mines are treated as separate sites for cleanup by the agencies in charge of restoration, reclamation, and reparation. Each one is considered a separate "case" so that nobody ends up seeing the problem holistically, if they see it at all. And nobody knows where the money will come from to take care of a problem this big. There's simply not enough to go around. "The US makes choices about how to spend its wealth," Shuey says, "and we've made some bad choices." As an example, he cites the expense of foreign wars that drain the coffers of funds that might be allocated to improving public health. Health is viewed as a commodity, he says—rather than, say, an inalienable right (an element of life, liberty, and the pursuit of happiness) or even a necessity—and today it's a commodity that many people cannot afford.

Ninety percent of the SRIC's resources are expended on legacy issues—documenting and seeking help to remediate the damage to people's land and bodies. The other 10 percent, says Shuey, goes to countering arguments for starting the mining all over again. Uranium mining was banned in the Navajo Nation when the Diné Natural Resources Protection Act was passed by the Tribal Council and signed by the tribal chairman in 2005. But there's been steady pressure, from outside and inside, to repeal the ban for the sake of economic relief if nothing else, even though "no Navajo family has ever made a fortune on uranium mining," according to Shuey, and many have instead suffered the kind of health effects that are notoriously hard to document,

1. Some authors use the term *Dinétah*, but according to memoirist Jim Kristofic, this is a mistake. *Diné Bikéyah* is used "to refer to all the land within the four sacred mountains in Colorado, New Mexico, and Arizona. Not to be confused with *Dinétah*, which refers to the original Navajo country, near Chaco Canyon in New Mexico" (Kristofic, *Navajos Wear Nikes*, 198).

Fence surrounding cleanup site

especially since health histories are often incomplete. The kind of studies now being done should have been done fifty years ago, in Shuey's opinion, but organizations such as the Indian Health Service were part of the problem rather than the solution; like everyone else, they purveyed the idea that uranium was good for the people and the nation. They participated in a massive program of denial.

As a journalist, Shuey tried to sell the story of contamination and accidents like the big one at Church Rock in 1979 to major news outlets, even "lefty publications" like *Mother Jones*, only to be turned away because his evidence for long-term damage did not seem strong enough. The editors, who were all members of the generation that survived the Great Depression and World War II—the Greatest Generation, it's been called—were inclined to trust that the government had the people's best interests at heart. Shuey came to believe that the journalists' old truism that there are two sides to every story and that both sides deserve a hearing was mostly a joke in practice. The writers and editors of the papers and magazines were not immune to socialization and not inclined to acknowledge radically different viewpoints. Since then, things have changed a little, in Shuey's view, thanks largely to the environmental movement, growing sympathy for the plight of indigenous peoples, and the slight drift of public opinion in acknowledging that a problem exists. Certainly nobody is claiming that uranium mining is harmless or patriotic anymore. And nothing that is readily found these days on government websites or in up-to-date reports from the agencies contradicts Shuey's testimony.

So the history of the Atomic Age has been longer and deeper than the history of the Manhattan Project. And, with its nuclear legacy, New Mexico has a yet stronger claim on the status of microcosm for the rest of the planet. Nuclear power has left traces almost everywhere, although because of remoteness and the passage of time, the trail to some locations becomes fainter. To follow the trail, the nuclear tourist must go beyond the famous historical sites to the more obscure crannies of Nuclear New Mexico, like the Grants Mineral Belt and the Four Corners region. Here the Cold War has definitely left its ruins: contaminated mining sites, abandoned towns, devastated lands, a legacy of illness, and not a little bitterness.

The bitterness suggests that the conjunction of Nuclear New Mexico with Indian country may be no less accidental than the conjunction of test sites and national labs with nature preserves. The federal government is deeply invested in all these places. The same is true for locations with reputations for alien encounters and conspiracy theories. Roswell is the most notorious, but northwestern New Mexico also participates, in places like Aztec in the Four Corners, where there was a reputed alien crash site much like Roswell's; and Dulce, where sightings of strange lights occurred in or near the Jicarilla Apache Reservation along with, oddest of all, unexplained cattle mutilations that have puzzled local residents for decades. Oh yes, even UFO aficionados find something of interest on the nuke tour.

Beyond the registered historical sites and national monuments, then, lies the shadow tour of Nuclear New Mexico. Here, instead of roadside markers with their official histories, shiny displays in government-sponsored museums, novels by best-selling authors, and documentary films, you must take as your guides the poets and storytellers who draw on the oral traditions of indigenous peoples, the testimony of activists, the reports of investigative journalists, even the tall tales of cranks and conspiracy theorists. Now, along with archaeotourism and ecotourism, nuclear tourism overlaps with "toxic tourism."[2] Nature is just as appealing, and the sun shines just as brightly in the stops on the shadow tour, but history tends to fade away, and the land is slower to give up its secrets. Prepare to take a hard look.

2. See Phaedra C. Pezzullo's book *Toxic Tourism: Rhetorics of Pollution, Travel, and Environmental Justice*. Pezzulo analyzes available tours of toxic sites in Louisiana (Cancer Alley), the Texas-Mexico border, and San Francisco.

Grants Mineral Belt

Acoma Pueblo

The shadow tour begins in the Grants Mineral Belt, also known as the Grants Uranium District. Take I-40 west from Albuquerque, cross the west mesa with its volcanic cones, and keep towering Mount Taylor in sight on your right. Before long, you'll come to the town of Grants, a place surrounded on every side by Indian country: the Sky City of Acoma Pueblo to the southeast, which offers mesa-top tours and spectacular views of Mount Taylor and the surrounding hill country, much of the scene scarred by open-pit mining and drilling for oil and gas; Laguna Pueblo on its little hill to the east, its sunrise-facing mission church surrounded by the stuccoed stone masonry of the village; and to the north, the expansive lands of Diné Bikéyah, the Navajo Nation.

Focus for a moment on the town of Grants itself. It has a story to tell about the world created by the discovery of nuclear power and about the movement of money and people in the extractive industries. Of course there are cities all over the country with dead downtowns killed by suburban flight. Small towns in the Midwest are abandoned when farm business goes belly up as soils wear out or weather turns bad for several seasons or markets dry up. Industrial cities in the North and mill villages in the Northeast and shallow South are left to antique dealers and curio shops when the automotive or textile industry moves overseas in search of ever-cheaper labor, leaving behind the ruins of economic warfare and a future of mechanization. But mining and oil patch towns are different. If you've ever lived in places like Midland, Texas, you know. It's boom and bust, with cyclic ups and downs that periodically attract a wandering tribe of miners, engineers, field hands, roughnecks, roustabouts, and capitalists. Local people join in while the money flows and then stay behind to pick up the pieces of a former life or move on with the rest of the migrants in search of the elusive dollar.

Grants, New Mexico, is such a place, its fortunes and failures governed by the market for mineral wealth. For some three decades, Grants was known as the Uranium Capital of the World. In 1950,

Paddy Martinez, a Navajo living in the area, became the subject of legend when he heard talk of prospectors searching for yellow-streaked rock and found a sample at the foot of Mount Taylor, a stone nearly covered with the bright yellow mineral. He took it to the assay office, and the rush was on. Companies poured in, and the mining and milling of uranium eventually led to more than four thousand jobs in the region. To the north, scientists at Los Alamos were no longer congratulating themselves on winning the world war but were locked in hot pursuit of what they called the Super, the hydrogen bomb, based on nuclear fusion, fighting the Cold War that followed the Soviet Union's successful test of atomic weaponry in 1949. They continued to search for more effective fission weapons as well, including the triggering devices for fusion bombs. Their work in the arms race and the whole machinery of nuclear proliferation fueled the demand for uranium. Grants lay strategically in the middle of things, with Los Alamos to the north, Sandia Labs just over the mountain to the east, the memory of Trinity to the southeast burned into the memory of the locals, and to the north and west, in Navajo country, an already active uranium-mining industry. Grants quickly rose to claim a share in the history of Nuclear New Mexico. Names of industry leaders like Anaconda and Kerr-McGee rolled off local tongues.

High unemployment in the region made cheap labor plentiful, according to the Acoma poet Simon Ortiz, who worked in the uranium-processing mills for a while in the 1950s. "In the decades before," he writes, "there was a small-scale timber industry, as well as some agricultural employment (mostly in picking and packing carrots), railroad work, and tourism, but nothing quite like this uranium boom." Acoma Pueblo as a whole, he says, "felt better off financially because of mining wages earned, though I noticed there was less attention given to gardens, fields, orchards, and livestock" (*Woven Stone*, 22). Native men were sometimes hired as strikebreakers when the union organizers came in, as Ortiz reveals in a poem called "Indians Sure Came in Handy":

During the organizing time
and during that strike in 1961,
that jail full of Indians sure came in handy.
The jailer would even call in sick for you
and tell you which mines were hiring Indians.
The Unions didn't have much of a chance,
and Grants just kept on booming. (297)

But, as Ortiz might be the first to tell you, the boom didn't last, and the mining took its toll on the people and the land.

Along with the arms race, the boom for uranium from 1950 until the late seventies was driven by the promise of peacetime uses, the growth of the nuclear power industry in particular, though the cost of uranium processing made the industry slow to develop, a venture that would have been impossible without government subsidies. "It takes a big power plant—enough to serve a city," John McPhee wrote in 1974, "just to run one gaseous diffusion plant [to make uranium usable]. The existing ones get their energy from power plants that burn strip-mined coal. Some people used to wonder aloud when the nuclear industry was going to produce more power than it was using, a question that was regarded by the industry as a 'sick joke'" (*Curve of Binding Energy*, 12). Northwestern New Mexico had the coal to burn as well as the uranium to fuel the plants. Money poured in despite the initial doubts.

But the doubts and worries began to pile up toward the end of the Cold War. In 1979 came the highly publicized Three Mile Island accident in Pennsylvania; in 1986, the Chernobyl meltdown; in 1989, the fall of the Soviet Union. Over the 1980s, there was a corresponding decline in the value of uranium. The companies began to pull out of Grants, the jobs to disappear. By the end of the decade, the economic gain of thirty years had all but disappeared. The boom town had gone bust.

These days, with the mining industry on long-term hold, Grants seems to support itself mainly as a stop on the interstate highway.

The Uranium Café
in Grants

The nearby El Malpais National Monument with its expansive ancient lava field and striking rock formations offers a fine stop on the map of Natural New Mexico, but the town seems to struggle to gain a foothold in the tourist trade. Cafés have a hard time getting enough business to stay open. The lurid green and yellow, out-of-commission neon sign for the Uranium Café still hangs in front of the boarded-up business, its other side given to the latest iteration of the restaurant, Badland Burgers, also closed. For the time being, you can still take a selfie with the sign in the background, but it's hard to say how long it will continue to hang as the building stands empty and dilapidated.

The café is across the street from the New Mexico Mining Museum, billed as "the only uranium mining museum in the world." It features a model underground mine that you reach via elevator. You can walk around down there and take pictures of rusty old equipment, hand-operated drills, ore cars on tracks, displays with Geiger counters, miners' lamps, hard hats, and other curiosities. The fading photographs on the walls show the equipment in action with miners at their work.

Back upstairs you can walk through the history of Grants from prehistoric times to the near present. You can admire a glass-enclosed display of local rocks and minerals, including a bright yellow sample of raw uranium "just like the one Paddy Martinez found." (You are free to wonder whether or not it is actually *radioactive* uranium.) You can learn about the uranium boom and the ultimate bust.

One curious display tells of the discovery of radioactivity and the various uses of elements like uranium. The more inane applications,

New Mexico Mining Museum

like the coloring of glassware, are explained by placards, but when it comes to weaponry, a photograph of the explosion at Trinity and another showing a nuclear submarine stand without even a note of identification. Some things, you may surmise, require no explanation, or are better left unsaid.

Like the Los Alamos Historical Museum, this one shows some signs of neglect and underfunding. The dusty and aging condition of the displays is as telling as the information provided. But unlike the Los Alamos Historical Museum, the one at Grants is not likely to get an infusion of funds when the money for national parks gets handed out. Right now, the compact building at 100 Iron Avenue has one of the snappier and best-maintained exteriors on the streets of

Drilling display and atomic symbol

ATOMIC SYMBOL
DONATED BY
Uranium Resources Inc.

Grants, standing in the middle of a handsome little park, its grounds decorated with big drilling structures and other artifacts of the industry. But like the rest of the town, it emits the feeling of an uncertain future.

Church Rock

As you go west from Grants, the story of the land and its people becomes ever more solemn as you come to the end of the Grants Mineral Belt. Just east of Gallup, you pass the village of Church Rock, north of Interstate 40 on the southern edge of the Navajo Nation (the part known as the "Big Rez"). This stop, like so many on the shadow tour of Nuclear New Mexico, seems almost pointless. There's not even a forlorn boomtown gone bust like Grants. There's no museum. Instead, it's an old industrial site, surrounded by stately sandstone mesas, left to lawsuits and cleanup. If you go too close to the fenced-off properties with the warning signs, you may find yourself followed by a red pickup truck that looks semiofficial.

But the point is not to find roadside attractions here or disrupt the business at hand, whatever it is. The point is to pay homage.

Church Rock is the site of the most damaging accident in the history of the US nuclear power industry, although at the time, few people outside New Mexico heard about it and few remember it today, even inside the state. Coming less than four months after the Pennsylvania mishap on March 28, 1979, the coverage of which made "Three Mile Island" (TMI) a catch phrase among newshounds, environmentalists, and nuclear watchdogs, the even more harmful accident at Church Rock dropped into the pond of public consciousness with barely a ripple. You would think that journalists would have rushed to the scene to follow up the TMI accident with this related story, but no. Neglect and ignorance were left to gather around this moment in the history of Nuclear New Mexico.

Old United Nuclear
Corporation (UNC) building
near Church Rock

United Nuclear Corporation Mill

The moment was July 16, 1979. At 5:30 a.m. that morning, at the uranium processing plant operated by United Nuclear Corporation, the mill tailings pond containing some one thousand tons of solid radioactive waste in solution breached the dam that held it in place. Before the leak was stopped at 8:00 a.m., ninety-three million gallons of the highly acidic and radioactive water had rushed into the Rio Puerco, a sizable stream that runs west from the Continental Divide into Arizona and the Little Colorado Watershed. The flood was big. It backed up sewers and seeped into aquifers as it passed through Gallup and on into Navajo County, Arizona, and Diné Bikéyah. Over eighty miles of the river were almost immediately rendered unfit for use. The largely Navajo population in the rural surrounding areas, who depended on the river for irrigation and cattle watering, were exposed to serious danger.

From that moment on, the state of New Mexico, the Navajo Nation, and the federal government have struggled to assign blame, determine the degree of damage, make reparations to the people, and reclaim the land, but it's been a complicated business. United Nuclear removed tons of contaminated riverbed before the company closed its facilities in 1982 when uranium prices plummeted. As the company phased out its efforts, various government agencies have continued the cleanup to the present day.

Today you can read about Church Rock on the internet, but the story has been slow to come out. The first journalists who tried to break the story, including young Chris Shuey, found their publication outlets uninterested. "Show me the bodies" sums up the attitude of many editors in those days. Like most people in the West, they generally trusted the government and the companies to take care of business in a reasonable manner, and if anything, they were grateful to the military-industrial complex for winning the world war and continuing to provide jobs in a state where money was sometimes scarce. Environmentalist attitudes were not nearly as widespread then as now, and the low population of the region, not to mention the neglect of indigenous people, made the event less newsworthy than the

Three Mile Island accident (Shuey, interview; see also Killingsworth, *Facing It*).

As you watch the river flow on your stop in Church Rock or Gallup or in the Painted Desert to the west, here are a few choice facts to remember:

- The radiation released at Three Mile Island was estimated at thirteen curies, while the Church Rock spill released some forty-six curies, but the national press made Three Mile Island a cause célèbre while ignoring Church Rock altogether.
- A USGS study found that the health impact at Church Rock was difficult to assess because the Rio Puerco had been contaminated for decades by "discharges of untreated or poorly treated uranium mine water and municipal sewage," and "impacts attributable to the tailings spill and mine dewatering could not be determined independent of contributions from natural conditions by the early 1990s" (SRIC, "Church Rock," 1).
- The Rio Puerco served as the catchment zone for the local Navajo people, who, as Valerie Kuletz points out, "were unable safely to use their single source of water, nor could they sell or eat the livestock that drank from this water" (*Tainted Desert*, 26–27). Public health officials who studied the case often had little understanding of how deeply the people depended on the river. In Pasternak's exposé, "the authorities' ignorance of the way Navajos live" is evident in their advice that eating the meat of exposed animals "would not pose a problem *so long as the people there didn't depend on the butchered animal for their everyday food over a long period of time*" (*Yellow Dirt*, 150, Pasternak's italics). The obvious assumption is that the people have some source of meat other than their own livestock, but the regional Navajos couldn't always just pop down to the supermarket to buy beef imported from Texas or Argentina. There often wasn't enough money. The Centers for Disease Control concluded that "federal exposure standards for the

general public would be exceeded when livers and kidneys of exposed cattle were eaten over a fifty year period," but the report failed to recognize that "liver and kidney meats are regularly eaten by Navajos, particularly the elderly for whom such 'choice' meats are provided" (Robinson, "Uranium Production," 182).

- Besides being a key source of water, the Rio Puerco was central to the community in other ways: "Local medicine men derived remedies from the native plants that grew along the riverbank, and children played in the river during hot summer months" (Brugge, deLemos, and Bul, "Sequoyah Corporation," 1597).
- "Incidents in low-income, rural American Indian communities have not attracted the same attention as have incidents in communities of higher socioeconomic status such as Three Mile Island or incidents that affected White victims such as Karen Silkwood" (Brugge, deLemos, and Bul, "Sequoyah Corporation," 1599).

No wonder cynical observers are quick to point out that Indian lands are often located close to nuclear sites and military installations and thus serve as a buffer zone that can be more easily kept out of the news and away from public scrutiny, much like the government-controlled nature preserves that also seem to crop up in such locations. Then again, most Indian tribes that managed to get reservations assigned close to their native lands, like most national parks and the largest acreages of public lands, are located in the West. And as Valerie Kuletz says, "the desert lands of the southwest United States have been transformed into arguably the largest peacetime militarized zone on earth . . . to what, in essence, is a military occupation." The signs are everywhere: "high-wire fences, radar antennae, massive satellite communication dishes . . . sonic booms, stealth aircraft, well maintained roads in the middle of 'nowhere' leading to various 'installations'" (*Tainted Desert*, 38–40).

Just another day, another stop on the shadow tour.

Four Corners

Canyon de Chelly National
Monument, Chinle,
Arizona

To drive further into the story of uranium mining on Indian lands, you'll want to stretch the boundaries of Nuclear New Mexico, heading west and north from Church Rock deep into Diné Bikéyah. From Gallup, take Highway 264 west and then turn north on 191.

You've crossed into Arizona now but remain within the boundaries of the Navajo Nation. Borders get fuzzy around here, like mirages on the road ahead. In the Four Corners, you're never far from switching states and are almost always within the borders of an Indian reservation—Navajo, Hopi, or Ute. It's appropriate for this arid land that rivers, mountains, and rock formations seem to mean more than state lines to the traveler. The Rio Puerco, which bears the mark of the Church Rock disaster, forms the southern boundary of the "Big Rez" of the Navajo Nation (with other segments of the nation off to the south and southeast). The San Juan River, to whose similarly troubled drainage you're headed now, forms the northern boundary.

On the way, you can stop to admire the wild cliffs and browse the archaeological sites at Canyon de Chelly, one of several remote but still frequently visited tribal parks administered by the Navajo Nation. The sinuous lines and bold contrasts revealed in the canyon's formations, as well as the people who live in its vicinity, have been immortalized by many celebrated photographers and painters, among them the late R. C. Gorman (who in his prime was that rare phenomenon, a Navajo celebrity).

If you skip the canyon, at least pull over for a break on the nearly deserted highways. Breathe in the dry air—clear your sinuses and your head among the dizzyingly abrupt mesas and buttes built of sandstone ranging in hue from ivory to deep maroon.

Follow 191 north into Utah and then turn west on 163. Before long, the wind-sculpted towers of Monument Valley appear on the horizon, one of the most famous destinations in the western United States, and certainly one of the most remote.

Its fame, at least among non-Indians, comes mainly from the efforts of one man, the entrepreneur Harry Goulding. A trader and sheepherder, Goulding ventured to Monument Valley with his wife,

Cliff dwellings, Canyon de Chelly

Monument
Valley on the
horizon

Goulding Museum (formerly Trading Post),
Monument Valley, Utah

called "Mike," in the early 1920s. Drawn by the beauty of the place and the grazing lands, Goulding noticed the obvious lack of nearby provisions to support the local Navajos. Opportunity was written all over the place.

He went to work as a provisioner in 1925, managing to cut a deal that allowed him first to lease, then to buy a patch of land from the state of Utah right in the middle of Diné Bikéyah, a well-placed outpost surrounded on every side by tribal lands. Things were sometimes touchy with the neighbors. Early on, many of them resented the competition from the Anglo's sheep herd. After he was forced to move his animals north in a federal livestock-reduction program that also removed or destroyed great numbers of Navajo sheep on the reservation (to relieve this overgrazed rangeland), he founded a trading post, beginning as a tent camp. The tents were soon replaced by a two-story building—the first multistoried structure that most of his Navajo neighbors had ever seen. Built from the local stone, it featured a pawnshop and general store on the first floor and living quarters on the second. In the north-side shade of a massive sandstone bluff, the post eventually grew to include a comfortable lodge that stands to this day and serves tourists from all over the world. The Goulding property also includes guest cabins, a campground, a good restaurant, a curio shop, and a big touring business. The original trading post is now a museum. Most of the employees are Navajo, which has been the case from the start. The Gouldings brought work and money to the local people living largely in poverty. A plaque in the museum lists the recipients of an annual educational scholarship funded by the Gouldings, along with letters from appreciative young Navajos and their pictures in graduation regalia.

The Gouldings succeeded pretty well in their early efforts—became rich by local standards—and even weathered the Great Depression without devastating losses. But things really took off in the late thirties when Goulding got the bright idea to sell the stark beauty of Monument Valley. He went to Hollywood and somehow finagled a meeting with the celebrated director John Ford to pitch the idea of

View from Goulding's
Lodge dining room

making westerns against a natural backdrop of blue sky and red rock. Ford bought it. He advanced the cash for Goulding to build barracks for crew and cast—the first "lodge"—and within weeks Ford was on site, making the movie that launched the career of John Wayne. *Stagecoach* transformed the genre of the western, replacing papier-mâché boulders and studio-yard sets with authentic natural landscapes that captivated audiences worldwide.

As the investigative journalist Judy Pasternak writes, "Goulding's successful maneuvering to purchase his private land in the middle of the reservation had proved his eye for the main chance" (*Yellow Dirt*, 34). When John Ford was summoned to make propaganda films for the armed services during World War II and had to suspend filming in Monument Valley, Goulding (a veteran of the army engineers in the World War I era) decided to do his part as well—and keep the money flowing his way in the process.

He worked as a kind of advance scout in the hunt for wartime resources, first for vanadium and then for uranium. Again, he was able to get jobs and much-needed income for his Navajo neighbors, who would as a result have more money to buy provisions from his store. For the Indians who "disapproved of ripping the innards out of Mother Earth," Goulding had crafted a special appeal: "The *leetso* [yellow ore] is the same color as the corn pollen. . . . You could put 'em side by side and you couldn't tell 'em apart. . . . We need that yellow dirt because it is strong like the pollen, and it makes bullets and helps in the war so much" (Pasternak, *Yellow Dirt*, 46).

The appeal eventually overcame all resistance, but it was a hard sell at first. The older generation still recalled stories of the Long Walk in 1858, when the Navajos were displaced from Diné Bikéyah and forced to live in exile at Bosque Redondo near Fort Sumner—their herds and orchards destroyed by Kit Carson and the US Cavalry—while the territorial governor of New Mexico followed up on rumors of gold deposits in the region (Locke, *Book of the Navajo*, 352). In 1868, the gold prospects having proved nonexistent, the Navajos were allowed to return, with bitter memories that have lingered into the new century. The mistrust was associated with mining and the hunger for resources among the Anglos. The word *leetso* was a little too close to Yeetso, the name of the big monster slain by the legendary twin sons of the great mother Changing Woman (Brugge, Benally, and Yazzie-Lewis, *Navajo People*, 6). In this legend, the monster's blood gave the rock of this country its reddish stain. Another tale from Navajo lore may have come into play as well—an origin story. When the people came from the third world into the fourth and present world, the gods bid them choose between two yellow powders—yellow dust from the rocks and corn pollen. They chose corn pollen and were commended by the gods but were also warned: Let the yellow dust remain in the earth. If removed, it will bring evil into the world (Eichstaedt, *If You Poison Us*, 47; see also Brugge, Benally, and Yazzie-Lewis, *Navajo People*, 105).

If not the devotion to the old legends, certainly the memory of the Long Walk was fading among the younger Navajos, who, against the advice of their elders, were attracted by the trader's promises of personal wealth and patriotic glory. They helped Goulding and the men he brought in from government-subsidized companies like the Vanadium Corporation of America locate the yellow dirt. They were rewarded by being favored for jobs when the mines opened, though questions about finder's fees and similar disputes plagued the relationship, foreshadowing even darker moments to come. By 1943, uranium from Navajo lands became part of the supply that fed the secret project in Los Alamos.

Goulding's entrepreneurial spirit made him the exclusive local service host for the Hollywood filmmakers and the mining companies with their military connections, as well as banker and provisioner to the Navajos, their go-between with the outside world where the world war raged. He and Mike profited nicely from the arrangement, and a few of his Navajo companions did okay as well. But the Navajos in the region, according to the story as told by the journalists and activists, have never recovered from the damage to land and health incurred by the uranium mining. It wasn't long before lung cancer began to appear regularly among the miners working in relatively crude conditions, with poor ventilation and failure to abide by best practices for avoiding prolonged contact with uranium dust and radon gas. Not as much was known then as now about such matters, but Pasternak offers good evidence to show that health concerns were back-burnered in the rush to provide uranium, first for the war effort and then, after 1949, for the Cold War proliferation of nuclear arms and experiments in peacetime nuclear technology (see also Udall, *Myths of August*, chap. 9, "The Betrayal of the Uranium Miners"). In addition to the rise in cancer cases among miners themselves, the legacy took on a genetic aspect and continues today as doctors and

Goulding's Lodge
stagecoach and saloon

government officials try to sort out the causes of birth defects and other long-term health problems.

If you don't mind supporting the Goulding legacy, you can book one of the rather expensive and much-in-demand modest rooms at the lodge, enjoy a Navajo taco or another treat featuring the local fry bread in the restaurant, feast on the nostalgia of the wars and movies of the Greatest Generation, and visit the museum on site, all within view of the hallucinatory formations of Monument Valley.

The legacy the Gouldings valued most—their pride in the beauty of Monument Valley, their patriotic contribution to the war effort, their neighborliness to the Navajos—is on full display in the old trading-post building. The museum's film room is the largest and best pre-

THE SHADOW TOUR

served, featuring movie posters, production shots, and on-location photos of the stars and movie makers, beginning with Ford and his casts and coming down through such films as *The Eiger Sanction*, *Thelma and Louise*, *The Wild, Wild West* with Will T. Smith, and *The Lone Ranger* with Johnny Depp. You realize that the celebrities from the world of cinema who have come to Monument Valley following Goulding's lead span three generations. In other parts of the museum, famous authors like Zane Grey are portrayed during their visits to the site.

You have to look harder for the uranium story. Tucked into a corner of the Josef Muench Room (honoring the noted photographer who came to Monument Valley to add to its internationally recognized iconicity), you'll find two black-and-white shots by unknown photographers. One is called *Uranium Survey Team 1950s*. It depicts an undistinguished group of men in dungarees, khaki shirts, and wide-brimmed hats. They could be mining for anything or even surveying locations for new movies. The other photo, copyrighted for a story in *Time* magazine about the uranium rush and titled *Testing for Uranium*, is more telling. Harry Goulding points a Geiger counter at a rock held bare handed by a Navajo man in straw hat and sunglasses, identified as Harry Benally. The man's wife, Anita, stands in the background in what seems a wary posture, with one child in her arms, two more standing close beside her. In both images, the sculpted rocks of Monument Valley, Utah, rise behind the human subjects, as if bearing witness on behalf of Nature.[3]

On the same wall is a larger display devoted to the World War II heroes who foiled Japanese radio spies by sending Allied messages in Diné, a language unidentifiable to America's enemies. The placement of the two displays—one on either side of the door leading out of the Muench Room—suggests a strong continuity between the work of the celebrated Code Talkers and the work of the uranium prospectors—a rhetorical relic of the old rationalizations for prospecting and mining the *leetso*.

Above all else, the images of the museum celebrate the lives of

3. Your guides wondered whether there were other photos pertaining to uranium that were not on display. The lodge manager obligingly opened the Goulding archives to us. We found only one other relevant shot, which depicted the search for uranium and was very much like the one on display, but this one was credited to Josef Muench. Then, as now, the history of uranium mining in the region was weakly documented compared to other activities. In this sense, Judy Pasternak's detailed story proves all the more valuable and impressive.

Harry and Mike Goulding. The many pictures of the couple show them in various activities at different stages of life—standing by their tents as they establish the trading post, overseeing construction of the red-rock trading post, then inside the building, bargaining for pawned jewelry and Navajo blankets, mingling with their neighbors and clients among the Diné, posing with government leaders like Arizona senator Barry Goldwater or Hollywood celebrities like John Ford and John Wayne—but most often out on the land, cooking over a low fire Navajo style, riding horseback, surveying, hiking, or just standing, smoking, looking.

You might reasonably imagine that Harry Goulding, though his love for the land was predominant, also loved people. A born trader and a good talker, he sought out all kinds of people and invited them onto his land and the land of his Navajo neighbors. He convinced the photographers and filmmakers of the valley's beauty until they came and came again. They paid him in full—not only in cash and customers, but also by making the place into a cultural icon.

And they still come. On any given day at Goulding's Lodge or in the nearby Navajo Tribal Park, you may meet parties from Japan, France, Germany, Italy, and the United Kingdom, flocking to see where John Wayne and Henry Fonda sat their horses against a backdrop of sculpted sandstone, a landscape of immense formations spread against the red land, backed by brilliant blue sky clarified and deepened by perennially dry air. The landscape says "West" to most people.

Among those whom Goulding invited to Monument Valley were the mineral prospectors seeking the metals that the world war made valuable: vanadium to make the steel stronger in the armor plating of naval vessels, and uranium to build the bomb and fuel the Atomic Age. Searching and mining for the metals did not leave iconic images for posterity and future tourism. The most impressive testimony appears in the museum in a letter from General Dwight David Eisenhower, praising the efforts of the Monument Valley Navajos in providing vanadium for the war effort. As Judy Pasternak explains, the letter came in response to a letter from Harry Goulding that told of the Navajos'

work and included their signatures, or rather their thumbprints, because most of them could not write in English. "I wish I could shake hands with every one of them," writes Eisenhower. The letter hangs on a second-story wall in the museum, in the preserved living quarters of the Gouldings, near the old upright piano (which had to have been an unmatched curiosity when it first came to Monument Valley).

Pasternak also explains that by the time Goulding and Eisenhower exchanged letters in 1943, the demand for vanadium was down, while the demand for uranium was on the rise. The two elements appeared together in the same ore, and the government had contracted with the vanadium companies to mine uranium and recover it from their vanadium mill tailings. "Vanadium" was practically a code word for uranium by then. Goulding himself, like many others involved in the industry, figured out that something secret and very important was going on with the uranium and had to be cautioned by federal agents to keep the lid on.

You can take a guided tour of the valley that leaves directly from

View of Monument Valley
from the gift shop in the
Navajo Tribal Park

the lodge. You can ride a bus or a horse. (You might overhear a British visitor complain that after taking the horseback tour, he found himself "walking just like John Wayne.") Or you can drive a few short miles to the Cultural Center operated by the tribe and tour from there. Be sure to pack your camera. The pros among the many photographers and filmmakers who have worked here will tell you that the fabulous contrasts and clear air make it nearly impossible to get a bad shot.

As you leave Monument Valley, musing on the legacy of the place as you head east on Highway 163, you might be surprised if you happen to stop near the village of Halchita, perhaps to photograph the continually stunning rock formations on this National Scenic Byway

THE SHADOW TOUR

or the small herds of wild burros that roam near the highway in search of good grass. Over the rise from the side of the road, you'll come upon what first appears to be a lake in the shimmering sunlight. You're close to the canyon-cutting San Juan River, so a dam and a small lake are not out of the question, even in this desert. However, closer inspection reveals that the feature is a wide field of gravel. No signs explain what's going on. Wild burros munch the thin grass nearby while you scratch your head and wonder.

A quick check of the internet will reveal that you have stumbled upon the Mexican Hat UMTRA site. UMTRA stands for Uranium Mill Tailings Remedial Action, a nationwide cleanup project involving several Four Corners sites, operated by the US Department of Energy (DOE) and funded by an act of Congress in 1978. The site near Halchita is an attempt to stabilize the tailings pile from the Mexican Hat uranium mill, which operated from 1956 through 1963, grinding ore and refining uranium to fuel Cold War initiatives. The 2.2 million tons of waste was not stabilized when the mill shut down and the sponsoring company pulled out, allowing the land to revert to the Navajo Nation. With groundwater and the nearby river threatened, the DOE intervened. A concrete cell was constructed with layers of insulation around the waste—not only Mexican Hat waste but also additional tonnage brought over from sites even closer to Monument Valley. The cell, with its two-foot-thick radon-infiltration barrier, is capped by multiple layers of protective material and is finished with a sand-and-gravel cover to allow safe drainage. It covers seventy-two acres and still radiates weakly, but no further action is planned. (See Rekow, "Monument Valley.")

Back in the car, headed east, you come to Mexican Hat Rock, the feature that gave its name to the village down the road and the uranium mill that operated there. You can take a good dirt road to get closer and then walk around the formation. Its funny name is surprisingly appropriate, a rare example of wit among the official names of natural sites. On the far side is a fine view of the San Juan River, the northern boundary of Diné Bikéyah. On its westward flow to Lake

Mexican Hat UMTRA
site, Halchita, Utah

Mexican Hat Rock

Lining up for pictures at the Four Corners Monument

Powell and the Colorado River, it passes many such sites, some visible like the UMTRA cell, but most hidden from view and inaccessible to the public, if not to the deer, the rodents, the birds, the burros, the cattle, the sheep, and yes, the people who live in this remote land.

Pressing eastward by one of several routes, you come to the Four Corners Monument, which you can see for a fee claimed by its Navajo hosts. The site marks the intersection of Arizona, Colorado, New Mexico, and Utah. People line up to touch four states at once.

Then drive on, taking US 64 across northernmost New Mexico. At the town of Shiprock, you enter an industrial corridor that includes the towns (west to east) of Kirtland, Fruitland, Farmington (the largest), and Bloomfield, with Aztec off a little to the north. On the edge of Diné Bikéyah, this center of resource extraction anchors the industry of northwestern New Mexico the way that Artesia anchors the southeast.

Just to the south of the town of Shiprock stands the volcanic formation of Ship Rock—or Rock with Wings as it's known to the Diné, a name that Tony Hillerman's daughter Anne adopted as the title to her recent novel, set partly in Monument Valley, the latest extension of the detective saga begun by her late father. Ship Rock is visible from all around the Four Corners, including an especially awe-inspiring vista from Mesa Verde near Cortez, Colorado. Its monumental beauty is not diminished even in comparison to the colossal Four Corners Generating Station in Fruitland, which was one of the largest coal-fired power plants in the world in its prime, large enough to have been seen by astronauts from space, a distinction it shares with the Great Wall of China. Controversy has always surrounded the generating station, which is leased from the Navajo Nation, as the various states vie for control of the electricity and environmentalists go to court, with some success, in claiming damage to air quality in Grand

THE SHADOW TOUR

Canyon National Park and other protected sites, as well as health risks for local populations, all protected by the Clean Air Act of 1963. The characteristic haze of the region sometimes obscures the view of Ship Rock, adding to the hallucinatory effect of the scenery, but recent years have witnessed the closing of some of the plant's units and new pollution controls on units that remain open. It's still dusty in the Four Corners but not as smoky as it once was, despite the two enormous generating stations that stand at the northeastern and northwestern corners of Diné Bikéyah—the Four Corners plant in Fruitland and the Navajo Generating Station in Page, Arizona. The towering smokestacks and power lines compete with the rivers and the four sacred peaks corresponding to the four cardinal directions— Mount Taylor (the south, near Grants), Mount Hesperus (the north, in western Colorado), Blanca Peak (the east, in the San Luis Valley of Colorado), and the San Francisco Peaks (the west, near Flagstaff, Arizona)—for the honor of defining the edges of Navajo country (both historical and mythic).

Highway 64 runs straight through the oil and gas fields and businesses devoted to them. If your appetite hasn't suffered, you can stop for "Serious Texas Bar-B-Q" or "Sooner BBQ"—the chosen cuisine of the oil patch and its wandering tribe.

Dulce

Keep driving east, and eventually the strip malls and service centers yield to winding roads in the forestlands and foothills of the San Juan Mountains. You can still see oil derricks and gas fields along the way, but by the time you reach the Jicarilla Apache Reservation, the pine forest predominates. You may be tempted to breathe a sigh of relief. But not so fast.

On the northern edge of Apache land, within shouting range of the Colorado border and abutting the Carson National Forest, Dulce appears on TV weather maps as one of the few identifiable towns in north-central New Mexico. It's a tiny gathering of humanity, tribal offices, schools, government housing, and pickup trucks. There are no national monuments, only a small state historical marker about the local Indians and a great deal of beautiful land on every side, plenty of standing timber, mainly ponderosa pine, and a skyline dominated by high ridges and green mesas.

You probably won't stop—nowhere really to eat or lodge, no easily accessible trailheads. But it's a perfect place if your intent is to hide secret government projects. The history of Dulce—supplemented by local legends and lore—suggests that just such a thing has happened, maybe more than once. The town has a significant place on the map of Nuclear New Mexico.

Dulce was the closest town to an operation known as Project Gasbuggy, part of the larger Project Plowshare. The mission was to find peacetime uses for the technology associated with nuclear weaponry (hence the biblical metaphor: beating swords into plowshares). On December 10, 1967, the El Paso Natural Gas Company, in collaboration with the Lawrence Radiation Laboratory and with funding from the Atomic Energy Commission, ignited an underground explosion to loosen a rock formation that hindered access to a large deposit of natural gas. The explosive device was an atomic bomb—a small one by the standards of those days, a twenty-nine-kiloton yield detonated at a depth of 4,227 feet. It produced a crater eighty feet wide and some three hundred feet deep, and up to a point, it worked. Wells were drilled and gas extracted. The problem was, the gas was too radioactive to be used for commercial purposes. Much of the ground had to be removed, the site leveled, and drilling and digging prohibited for the foreseeable future (Valdez, *Dulce Base*, 39–40). One schoolteacher in Dulce remembers the big tremor from the blast, twenty-eight miles away, that made everything in his classroom vibrate. It shook groceries off the shelf in a local store. A similar experiment was carried out in western Colorado in an attempt to refine the technique. But the entire set of operations lost funding and now stands as a bizarre subplot in the early history of fracking, as the technique is known

today. (The current method favors water and a variety of chemicals over atomic explosives; it's hydraulic fracturing rather than nuclear.)

The Gasbuggy site, about twenty-five miles southwest of Dulce, is roughly accessible via a dirt road (FS 357) leading into the Carson National Forest. It is commemorated by a historical marker and, at ground zero, a stone monument vaguely resembling something you might see in a cemetery, on which is mounted a metal plaque that briefly describes the project. (See "Gasbuggy Nuclear Test Site," Center for Land Use Interpretation.) A full-sized replica of the rig used for the Gasbuggy experiment is on display at the Aztec Museum and Pioneer Village, along with a collection of documents and photos related to the event.[4]

If you think the story can't get any weirder, think again. For years bizarre rumors have surrounded Dulce. Unexplained bright lights have appeared in the sky; mysterious marks on the ground. One of the local ridges was said to be hollowed out and used as a base—either aliens at work, or the US military, or both.

Then, strangest of all, in 1976—the nation's bicentennial year—the cattle mutilations began. Local ranchers found cows and other large

4. The exhibit was sponsored by museum board member Tom Dugan, who has been involved in gas and oil exploration in the San Juan Basin since 1948. Thanks to Dr. Jimmy Miller of San Juan College, also a board member, for calling our attention to the exhibit at the small municipal museum.

livestock dead in the fields, with their mouths, anuses, and genitals (and occasionally other organs and tissues) removed with what appeared to be bloodless surgical precision. No tracks, human or animal, led to the sites; no tracks led away. At some sites, there were only strange marks suggesting a heavy tripod and some evidence that the cattle had been taken away, perhaps to the hidden base nearby or even farther away to some secret laboratory for testing. No one could say. The cause of death was never clearly determined for many of the cattle, though blunt-force trauma was frequently blamed. The cattle did not seem to have fought or struggled.

Similar mutilations had been going on in the nearby San Luis Valley of Colorado for nearly a decade, beginning in 1967 with the case of Lady the Appaloosa mare (a.k.a. Snippy the horse; see Howe, *Alien Harvest*, 1–7). About the same time as the Dulce mutilations, reports from Texas and the Midwest came flowing in. Government officials, state and federal, were not always inclined to talk to the reporters and ordinary citizens involved (Greenwood, interview). In an age of cover-ups (such as the Watergate scandal that had recently ended the career of President Richard Nixon), the reluctance to share information naturally raised suspicions.

A state policeman named Gabe Valdez was called by friends with ranches near Dulce to investigate the phenomenon. His story, which continued in many cases across northern New Mexico, is told by his son Greg in *Dulce Base: The Truth and Evidence from the Case Files of Gabe Valdez*. The elder Valdez never solved the mystery, leaving local folks and internet conspiracy theorists to wonder: Predators? Government tests? Aliens? Witches? Vandals? The latter were ruled out because of the eventual scale of the phenomenon—which manifested across the United States and even worldwide—and the seeming sophistication of the mutilations, which also seemed to rule out animal predation and scavenging (though that theory was preferred by most official sources). Noting the proximity of Indian reservations and government labs—Los Alamos is only seventy-seven air miles from Dulce, for example—and offering evidence of an elaborate cover-up,

Ridges above Dulce

Greg Valdez favors the government theory. The particular body parts removed from the cattle suggest some concern with their possible contamination by radioactive exposure. Radioactivity could have drifted into the region on the prevailing southwestern winds. The federal government would have been one of the few entities with the resources to carry out the mutilations on a global scale.

Another author, Linda Moulton Howe, takes a global perspective in her documentary film *A Strange Harvest* and the follow-up book *Alien Harvest: Further Evidence Linking Human Abductions and Animal Mutilations to Alien Life Forms.* She links the cattle mutilations to similar conundrums, like crop circles, and obviously favors the alien theory, which has the virtue of being as difficult to disprove as it is to prove, though plenty of people have weighed in on both sides. It becomes a matter of faith.

But Howe doesn't neglect the government. She is convinced, as she writes in *Alien Harvest*, that "the US government knows a great deal about animal mutilations, human abductions and the aliens who have intruded on our planet" (133). One of her key inside sources claims that the government made a deal with the extraterrestrials: "The aliens could conduct animal mutilations and human abductions in exchange for teaching US experts about alien advanced technologies." Part of the agreement was to provide a base for the aliens' research: "That base was later identified . . . as underground Area 51 . . . near Las Vegas, Nevada. Another base under Mount Archuleta near Dulce, New Mexico has also been mentioned" (135n).

Phaedra Greenwood, a journalist who reported on the mutilations for five years for the *Taos (NM) News* (1995–2000), takes a somewhat more agnostic view. While acknowledging the preponderance of evidence offered by witnesses—and not just kooks and cranks, but salt-of-the-earth ranchers, law enforcement officers, and numerous others—Greenwood feels that none of the theories fully accounts for all the facts. "The deeper you look," she says, "the more mysterious it becomes."

Road sign referring to cattle abductions in northern New Mexico

With no easy answers but much to ponder, it's time to drive on. If you keep going east, along Highway 64 toward Taos, you'll pass the familiar road signs that warn of cattle on the highway, many of which have been modified by local wits. Above the image of the black cow on a yellow background hovers a silver flying saucer—a reference to the mystery that remains unsolved.

To pursue the mystery and its unexpected connection with Nuclear New Mexico, turn right on US 285 in Tres Piedras and drive the 250 miles southeast to Roswell, the mother ship of conspiracy theory, where people first began to ask the question: Aliens or the government, or the two conspiring together?

Roswell

Roswell lies along the Pecos River where the plains of eastern New Mexico rise into the more rugged elevations in the southernmost reaches of the Rocky Mountains. The place is a transition zone, mainly devoted to farming and ranching, a quiet town with few disturbances. A mild climate prevails, mostly sunny with moderate temperatures and only occasional high winds to stir up the dust in the spring.

But in the summer of 1947, two years after the explosion at Trinity (roughly a hundred miles due west of Roswell) and the bombs were dropped in Japan and everything changed, something actually happened to put Roswell on the map. A local rancher discovered the wreckage of what appeared to be a spacecraft just north of town, with bodies of its passengers strewn about the rocky landscape. The witness reported the crash site to the authorities, and a team of military investigators was dispatched from the Roswell Army Air Field to take charge. The area was cordoned off and restricted. Mysterious events followed, loads of things were spirited in and out, rumors arose of flights carrying bodies away to Washington, and other witnesses came forward to report sightings of strange objects and lights in the sky. Silence from the authorities in charge allowed the rumors to grow

On the road into Roswell

Artistic depiction in front
of the UFO Museum of the
1947 events in Roswell

and spread. The local newspaper reported that aliens had landed. The air force finally came out with a report that said it was nothing but a weather balloon mishap. Authorities said there was plenty of semise-cret research going on in the region, connected with the air base and new investigations into rocket flight, including the work of the famous rocket scientist Wernher Von Braun, the former Nazi who worked in New Mexico after the war and later with NASA. (A museum in his honor now operates in Roswell, which joins Alamogordo as another stop on the rocket-and-missile subtour.) The bodies at the site might have been crash-test dummies used in test rockets in advance of manned space flight—one of many might-have-beens spread by strategic leaking as well as official reports. Policy documents later uncovered argued that if alien beings had actually landed, secrecy would be justified by the kind of damage that such information could do to the social fabric of American life—the religious belief that human beings were unique as the universe's single advanced life form, for example, or the feeling of security among a people already threatened by Cold War enemies. The very possibility of enemies from outer space could cause widespread panic, the kind inspired by the realistic but fictional newscast of a Martian invasion in Orson Welles's 1938 radio play based on H. G. Wells's *War of the Worlds*. Worries over mass hysteria—the motive frequently offered as an explanation for how the normally sensible German people could have been persuaded by Nazi propaganda—made secrecy a default option among government policy makers in the postwar years.

But the notion of an alien landing proved hard to dispel, and investigations both publicly and privately funded, professional and amateur, continue to this day. The US military has been charged with covering up the truth of the matter. The incident and the alleged cover-up became the inspiration for the popular TV series *The X-Files*, as well as dozens of comics and graphic novels, a 1994 Hollywood film starring Kyle MacLachlan and Martin Sheen, called *Roswell*, and a 1999 TV series by the same name.

What is the truth of Roswell? You can join the flocks of amateur investigators and decide for yourself. Tour the privately funded, low-budget UFO Museum in the old movie theater on the main street of town. Have your picture taken with the model aliens and their smoking spaceship, or take a selfie with the plastic alien on life support. Enjoy the huge collection of historical alien memorabilia, the kind for sale not only in the museum gift shop but on every corner in Roswell, where the alien landing has become a big part of the local economy. Read the original news accounts on the museum's wall displays and see photographs of spaceship sightings and the counterbalancing photos showing how spaceship photos can be faked, cartoons about the event, artifacts ranging from a crash-test dummy used in experimental rocket flights at the time, to reconstructions of the metal foil used in weather balloons compared to the metals allegedly found at the crash site. You can go into the "research library" and peruse hundreds of books and articles about alien sightings in ancient times, about Roswell and related incidents, about conspiracies and cover-ups in theory and practice. There are old magazines and hand draw-

Alien encounters inside the UFO Museum

ings of aliens done by those who claim to be witnesses.

But don't neglect another element in the truth about Roswell: the connections with Nuclear New Mexico. Some are banal and historical. To take one example, an early player in the Manhattan Project, Edward U. Condon, once the director of the National Bureau of Standards, was appointed to a civilian panel to study UFOs and alien encounters at the University of Colorado in the 1950s—a fact you can learn by reading the articles on display in the museum library. But a more important connection between places like Los Alamos and Roswell is the imaginative nexus, which may require you to fire up your own imagination.Consider, for example, the possibility that the aliens did come. They may have been drawn to New Mexico because of its central position in the new human discovery of atomic power. Pilgrims from outer space, who had been watching the evolution of life on planet Earth for millennia, may have decided that the time had come for an intervention.

Or, if you prefer something less sensational, just look at Roswell as a hub for the ways that our thinking and attitudes have changed since Trinity. (And consider this: Our thinking may have changed so much that Professor Einstein would not even recognize it as thinking.)

For one thing, there was a surge in the science fictional imagination, a new sense of what was possible. With the discovery of atomic power and the successful explosion of the bomb, science caught up with science fiction and opened new horizons of possibility. The historian Richard Rhodes tells how the pioneering nuclear physicist Leo Szilard, a Hungarian colleague of Einstein, first traveled to London in 1929 in hopes of meeting the science-fiction pioneer H. G. Wells. The two men shared a dream "somehow to save the world" (Rhodes,

Making of the Atomic Bomb, 14). It was the literary man Wells who, in his prophetic novel of 1932, *The World Set Free*, first imagined the liberation of atomic energy, the possibility of atomic bombs, and the dire future of a second world war (Rhodes, *Making of the Atomic Bomb*, 24). The literary prophecy culminated in the historical Manhattan Project, and science turned the tables on literature. What had all seemed fantasy and idle speculation, even to an admiring reader of Wells like Szilard, was suddenly real. The revealed power of the atom inspired waves of new thinking about the capability of human beings to disturb the universe.

Another element in the new thinking involved the relationship of secrecy with power. The Manhattan Project proved that the government could operate in ways undetected by public scrutiny and conduct world-changing research and development in the process. Conspiracy theories and suspicion amounting to public paranoia became the order of the day. The government began to seem independent of the people. As Elaine Scarry has suggested, the emergence of a thermonuclear monarchy had already begun by 1947. The ability to make war, once the prerogative of the people's representatives in Congress, along with the eventual capability to destroy the world, was now in the hands of one person, the president, and a handful of military advisers. A by-product of the bomb's antidemocratic thrust is the rampant mistrust of the government by the people and their own, forgive the pun, alienation.

This complex of attitudes and ways of thinking—the heightened imagination brought on by the atomic bomb, government secrecy, conspiracy theories, and public paranoia—plays out in the meme now called *Roswell*. In the actual town, a plastic green alien greets you at every stop. At one motel, a tiled floor on the elevator shows the familiar green face with the words "Welcome to Roswell, Earthlings." A collection of DVDs behind the desk at another motel features famous alien movies, from the Cold War classic *Invasion of the Body Snatchers* to the more recent *Cowboys and Aliens*, a good choice if you want something that resonates with the southwestern landscape

Roswell doorway

where ranchers stumble upon downed spacecraft, presumably containing the extraterrestrial enemy—the destroyer of worlds. A card in the motel bathroom urges you to "Save the Planet"—but wait: that's no different from every other motel in practically every town in the United States, where the message appeals to your ecological conscience but really means "don't make us wash your towel tonight." It also says to be a hero, a savior, not a destroyer of worlds.

Valley of Fires

If it all becomes too much, take your aching conscience, overplayed nostalgia, and supercharged sense of irony out to nature (which you've helped to save anyway by hanging your towel on the rack for a couple of days). Drive west on US 380. You're barely out of Roswell when the snowy cap of Sierra Blanca rises before your grateful eyes, the sacred home of the Mescalero Apaches. Pronghorns stroll into view as you climb into the hills from the grassy plains. Red-tailed hawks and perhaps a golden eagle soar in the air. Was that a UFO? No, it was a kestrel hovering over its prey, the little falcon that the English poet Gerard Manley Hopkins celebrated as a figure of the risen Christ in his poem "The Windhover." Perhaps you will breathe a prayer in your own way, to nature if nothing else, for relief from the plaguing thoughts of Nuclear New Mexico.

Drive on through the charming pastoral valley of the Hondo River where horses graze in mesa-bordered pastures, through the historical town of Lincoln with its Billy the Kid museum, through Capitan, home of Smokey the Bear, the villages redolent with frontier flavor. Cross the pass through the Sacramento Mountains in the shadow of Sierra Blanca, and enter the Valley of Fires.

In the narrow basin between the Sacramentos and the smaller Oscura range to the west lies the malpais or badlands, an ancient basaltic lava flow that vented out and covered a stretch of ground barely a mile wide and some fifteen miles long. (A similar but much larger and more complex feature lies near Grants at El Malpais.) There's a Bureau of Land Management (BLM) park in the Valley of Fires where you can camp or at least stop to take a looping nature trail on asphalt that matches the black basalt. The basalt still retains its molten twists and turns and still gives the feeling of flowing liquid rock frozen in time.

Plants reclaim the desert

The tougher plants of the desert have begun to reclaim the place. Sotol and yucca, barrel cactus and prickly pear, mesquite and native grasses find a niche in soils spared by the lava or blown in by the high winds of spring. Among the plants and in the curves and caves carved by the flowing rock, the animals have returned: collared lizard, bull snake, quail, mice, and mule deer, insects in the blossoms of yucca, arachnids hunting the flies and little bees. And thanks to the BLM, the people have also come back to this forsaken land, pilgrims with their sturdy shoes, the careful ones who cling to the path provided by the government, as well as the braver who risk a sliced boot or twisted ankle out in the rugged old lava flows. Even on the path, step with caution, for the prairie rattlers enjoy the warmth of the open pavement in winter and spring and the shade of the saltbush along the way in summer and fall. Listen for the rattle and catch a glimpse of the elegant serpent before it slides over the low wall on the side of the footpath.

Stand and gaze on what the heat of the lava can do and how life can recover itself in the harshest conditions. Remember that over those low hills to the west is Trinity Site, where human beings first made a second sunrise and melted sand into a glassy mineral with pseudovolcanic heat. Behind you, to the east, the aliens may have landed in the unlikely place called Roswell.

Valley of Fires

Collared lizard in
Valley of Fires

Everything changed, but life presses on in the age of nuclear power and global climate change. We seek a foothold and hang on tight, knowing that on the horizon, the next explosion or disaster awaits. We keep returning after the volcano but keep pushing the limit, seeking the line where earth meets sky. And what will we find, should we ever arrive?

The Literary Tour

3

Your tour guides offer this brief excursion into the terrain of literature and related arts as a supplement to other cultural references in the tour. You've landed among English professors, and well, that's what they do.

But without the literary angle, the tour may seem incomplete. Metaphors again: the mental or interior world of literature reflects and transfigures the outer world. It brings new imaginative perspectives to the historical tour, and it becomes the shadow of the shadow tour. It is colorful and Promethean down one road, dark and Faustian down the other. The roads often grow indistinct and merge in surprising ways.

In the event that your tour is fully virtual rather than physical, or if you find yourself at a motel or campground on the physical tour with free time to read, the literary tour provides additions to your reading list, along with commentary that connects the themes and characters of the reading. The tour branches in two directions. The first explores the influence of the atomic bomb on comics, graphic novels, and superhero movies. The second delves into exceptional novels and poems portraying the life of the people who continue to make their home in Nuclear New Mexico.

The Epic Literature of Modern Times; or See You in the Funny Papers

Spiderman is perhaps the most popular superhero of our day. Like many other comic-book and movie superheroes, he got his powers from a nuclear accident—the bite of a spider inadvertently irradiated in a laboratory setting.

Everybody knows about Spiderman, but what about his Navajo counterpart, Muttonman? The mock hero of a sporadic comic strip contributed to the *Navajo Times* by Vincent Craig beginning on February 12, 1981, Muttonman was an ordinary sheepherder until he contracted "limited" powers from eating mutton contaminated by the Church Rock spill. Then he became "helper of the weak, suppressor of bureaucrats, and all around good guy" (Craig, *Muttonman*, February 19, 1981): "faster than a jackrabbit, more powerful than the BIA [Bureau of Indian Affairs], able to leap Shiprock in a single bound" (Craig, June 25, 1981; see also Szasz, *Atomic Comics*, 125; Brugge, Benally, and Yazzie-Lewis, *Navajo People*, 4). Muttonman's costume is patched together from his grandfather's old football helmet, an old rug from a secret girlfriend, a few good-luck feathers and a letter from his nephew's high school letter jacket, a cheap T-shirt from a tourist shop, a concho belt won from a tribal councilman, a mask, and moccasins ("tenni-shoes").

Although Craig loosely patterned his character after Superman, he did so with characteristic Navajo humor and a political bite. Muttonman's primary charge was to help the Navajo people (and others) to "prevent another 'long walk' or other injustice" (Craig, February 26, 1981). In reflecting on the origin of Muttonman, Craig recalls a conversation with his father, a World War II Code Talker,[1] where they decided that Muttonman's powers had to be limited: it's "the destiny of Indians: that their powers will always have limitations. . . . That he's

1. Craig, a native of the Crownpoint area just north of Church Rock, was convinced that a melanoma that developed on his father's foot was a result of wading in the contaminated Rio Puerco. Vincent himself died of cancer in 2010

only going to be able to fly for five minutes, and he has to do everything in five minutes" (Del Mauro, "Vincent Craig's Secrets").

Despite his unfailing humor, Craig tackled such tough issues as the effects of radioactive contamination on livestock, frogs (sacred to the Navajos), and indigenous people; delaying efforts to obtain assistance from government agencies in the testing and cleanup of contaminated sites; government treatment of Vietnam veterans; even global biological warfare. In a 1981 comic strip sequence, a Russian satellite carrying a scientific experiment using "expansion bacteria" crashes into a hogan, releasing a dough-like substance that immediately engulfs a tourist RV. Called the frybread monster by the Navajos, it becomes Muttonman's nemesis. In a 1992 sequence, thirteen years after the Church Rock uranium spill that contaminated the Rio Puerco, Navajo youths discover a tree with softball-sized piñon nuts and a frog with two extra legs. Muttonman is subsequently charged by the tribal council to fly (under his own powers, of course) to Washington, DC, to learn the status of the paperwork pertaining to applications for government testing and cleanup of contaminated sites. But alas, when he finally opens the door to the correct office, he discovers that it contains an actual black hole engulfing entire stacks of paper.

Muttonman, "helper of the weak, suppressor of bureaucrats, and all around good guy" (Craig, February 19, 1981; use granted by *Navajo Times*, Window Rock, Arizona)

Spiderman and Muttonman share a place in the history of comics, graphic novels, and superhero films, which arguably comprise the epic literature of our times. In the vision of this literature, nuclear power has become the sword, the magic, and the source of the most formidable power. The table display of atomic-themed comic books in the culture room of the National Museum of Nuclear Science and History in Albuquerque shows how deeply the Nuclear Age has penetrated popular entertainment. The comics are covered with glass, so you can't thumb through the stories, but the colorful covers and provocative titles have an eloquence of their own. Here you find the animal fables of modern times, like *Atomic Rabbit* (1955) and *Atom-*

Muttonman comic strip, "What happened to the paperwork?" (Craig, September 3, 1992; use granted by *Navajo Times*, Window Rock, Arizona)

ic Mouse (1961); educational nonfiction striving to deflect the terror and dispel the confusion, revealing the mysteries and promise of the atom, including official government publications, and some bordering on the ridiculous, like *Dagwood Splits the Atom* (1949); and above all, the superhero tales, such as the October 1946 encapsulation of postwar fears, "Captain Marvel Battles the Dread Nuclear War." The comics are mainly American, but also included in the exhibit is *Gen of Hiroshima*, number 1, by the acclaimed Japanese pioneer of the graphic novel, Keiji Nakazawa. In the early 1970s, this became the several volumes of *Barefoot Gen*, now an international cult classic.

In American comics, the world-saving or Promethean side of atomic science gets worked out in the figure of the superhero. For a lively study of the shared history of nuclear power and comic-book heroism, have a look at *Atomic Comics* by the late Ferenc Morton Szasz, formerly a professor of history at the University of New Mexico. Professor Szasz's extensive collection of atomic-themed comics once formed a more extensive exhibit at the National Museum of Nuclear Science and History and was the inspiration for the current display.[2] Szasz's book shows that atomic science and the comic-book hero were connected virtually from the start. Although the ur-superhero, Superman himself, predates the bomb, several postwar episodes find the Man of Steel in adventures that involve the nuclear threat. In one issue on display in the museum, Superman goes journalist and covers an H-bomb test in the South Pacific. (You'd have to be invincible to get in close for good reporting without being obliterated like the target islands themselves!)

Immediately after the secrets of the atom became public information, a host of short-lived atomic superheroes sprang into being, along with the nonfiction comics devoted to educating the public on atomic issues. As Szasz points out, the educational prospects for atomic comics mostly fell flat while the entertainment potential proved a lasting key to success. Even so, the nonfiction tradition continues today with the publication of such titles as Jonathan Fetter-Vorm's 2012 *Trinity: A Graphic History of the First Atomic Bomb*, kind of a Classic Comics version of Richard Rhodes's densely informative histories. Rhodes's books, despite winning such accolades as the Pulitzer Prize and the National Book Award, are challenging to the point of impenetrability for many lay readers because of their detailed scientific explanations. Fetter-Vorm's graphic history fills the gap.

The old comic books usually err in the other direction—you know, dumbing it down and hamming it up. Reading the superhero comics in retrospect, you're likely to find the historical value more intriguing than any literary pleasure you might enjoy. In Szasz's estimation, "many modern nuclear-themed adventure tales treat the story of the

2. Unfortunately, the full collection is not currently available to the public, according to an email exchange with Professor Szasz's widow.

fissioned atom with such disdain, cynicism, or parody that they have helped create a pervasive gray atmosphere I term 'atomic banality'" (*Atomic Comics*, 5). A leading example of atomic banality is "the old reliable" among superhero plots: the nuclear accident (121). Superman was an immigrant like the parents of his creators, both of whom were second-generation German Jews (like Robert Oppenheimer, the father of the atomic bomb). The Jewishness of early comic heroes is venerated in Rabbi Simcha Weinstein's wonderfully titled study *Up, Up, and Oy Vey! How Jewish History, Culture, and Values Shaped the Comic Book Superheroes*. Superman's powers develop in the atmosphere of an alien planet, a reflection of the alien status that the many Jewish immigrant scientists experienced in America in their work on nuclear weaponry (like Edward Teller, the father of the hydrogen bomb). But the superheroes who came after Superman, as well as some villains, gain their powers when they are transformed by exposure to fissionable material or by knowledge of atomic secrets (or both). The stock plot emerged within months of the detonation of the first atomic bombs:

> In the November/December 1945 Headline Comics, Adam Mann accidently drinks a glass of heavy water into which some U-235 crystals had fallen. Then he stumbles into a high-voltage machine. This "incredible chemical accident" turns Adam Mann into a human atomic bomb, with the new power concentrated exclusively in his right hand. (He had to wear a lead glove to keep the radioactivity from leaking away.) Donning a red cape, a kilt, and a Roman legionnaire's helmet, "Atomic Man" spent his efforts righting various wrongs, such as thwarting a deranged scientist who planned to take over the world. (Szasz, *Atomic Comics*, 52)

The name Adam Mann is, of course, a double entendre, suggesting both Atom Man and the biblical character Adam, whose name in the context of the Hebrew Bible more or less means *man* or *mankind*. In the transformed world of atomic energy, Adam Mann is the new Adam, the atomic human. The genesis of the new human occurs not in the presence of God, but in the presence of the manipulated element U-235, which remakes humanity in its own image.

The allegory, or even the message, may have been too heavy for early postbomb readers. So soon after the war, people may have been weary of world-shaking conflict, even of good triumphing over evil. Or maybe the character was too silly a mix of the new superheroism with the ancient mythologies. Whatever the cause, Atomic Man lasted only six issues before being discontinued (Szasz, *Atomic Comics*, 53).

It was not until the second generation of atomic superheroes, in the 1960s, that nuclear transformation caught on fully, with characters more inclined to brood over their own powers or embody the contradictions of atomic energy. The reluctant hero Spiderman is the best example, but there are others. The Hulk, the alter ego of nuclear scientist Bruce Banner, appears after Banner is directly exposed in a laboratory accident, in a modern version of Dr. Jekyll and Mr. Hyde. The X-Men, mutants whose genes have been altered by a generation of radioactivity, continue the tradition of ambivalence (with characters like Wolverine mirroring the Hulk's unpredictability and others switching sides from the lawful to the criminal). The X-Men regularly encounter bands of villains with mutant powers like their own (perhaps a metaphor for the spread of nuclear weaponry to rogue nations). The godlike, if not altogether heroic, figure of Dr. Manhattan in Alan Moore's latter-day graphic novel *Watchmen* (1987) also follows the now-classic plot line, a nuclear scientist transformed into a walking atomic bomb and indestructible titan by careless laboratory procedures. From the comic master Stan Lee to the famous graphic novelist Alan Moore and the celebrated filmmaker Ang Lee, the creators of the superhero in pulp and celluloid have succeeded in capturing the popular imagination in ways that proved mostly out of reach to traditional literary forms like narrative poetry and literary fiction.

The history of comics offers the curious tourist a snapshot of the issue that nuclear historians and activists call *legacy*. What is the shape of the world inherited by the current generation from the so-called Greatest Generation, which survived first the Great Depression, then the war against fascism, and finally the Cold War, a world defined ultimately by the presence of atomic power and the possibility of complete annihilation of life by the human hand? As you've already seen, legacy issues plague medical studies that focus on increased cancer cases among uranium miners, workers exposed to radioactivity in power-plant accidents, and people living downwind from nuclear tests, not to mention the victims of the bombings in Japan, and the sons and daughters of irradiated parents. Similar accidents and issues of genetic legacy give us the modern superhero.

Legacy is treated with special poignancy in the recent history of superhero films. Some of Hollywood's most popular movies in the latest generation perpetuate the heritage of comic-book heroes and antiheroes transformed by nuclear accidents or genetic alterations caused by exposure: Spiderman, the Hulk, the X-Men, Dr. Manhattan. Then there's Iron Man, who, rather than making bombs as his father did, first makes a fortune on weaponry and then becomes a bomb himself—joining Dr. Manhattan as a successful version of the original atomic hero, Adam Mann. In this way, the tour of atomic comics brings us back to a prophecy from Late Atomic Culture, uttered by the novelist E. L. Doctorow. The bomb, says Doctorow, becomes "the great golem we have made against our enemies," but it eventually absorbs our identity, transforms our culture, and becomes the thing that best defines us as a people (quoted in Bird and Sherwin, *American Prometheus*, xii).

New Mexican Novels and Poems: The Power of Words and Witchery

The southwestern roots of atomic culture appear in the comics mainly by indirection. Desert landscapes, secret laboratories, and hollowed-out mountains abound. In Ang Lee's film version of the Hulk, the monstrous figure strides over a broad desert landscape to escape military aircraft hunting him down. Iron Man's father, we learn from hints in that film, worked at Los Alamos, and so on.

You can find a more direct connection with Nuclear New Mexico in traditional literature written by the state's own sons and daughters. In fact, you'd be hard pressed to find better writing on the topic than you can discover in the literary Landscape of Enchantment.

The best monuments to life and industry in the Grants Mineral Belt, for example, may well be literary, like Simon Ortiz's *Woven Stone* and Tony Hillerman's novel *People of Darkness*, a Jim Chee mystery set near Grants. Typical of Hillerman's highly successful Navajo police mysteries, this one educates as well as entertains the literary tourist. As you follow the adventures of the Navajo Tribal Police detectives, you learn a great deal about Diné metaphysics and mythic interpretations of the local land. Of Mount Taylor, for example, Hillerman writes:

> Tsoodzil, the Navajos called it, the Turquoise Mountain. It was one of the four sacred peaks which First Man had built to guard Dinetah. He had built it on a blue blanket carried up from the underworld, and decorated it with turquoise and blue flint. And he pinned it to the earth with a magic knife, and assigned Turquoise Girl to live there and Big Snake to guard her until the Fourth World ended. (29)

In *People of Darkness*, you'll also encounter names and incidents from the history of Nuclear New Mexico, including mention of the Anaconda Corporation, Kerr-McGee Nuclear Fuels, and the Red Deuce Mine: "the immense dusty hole" with "a dozen gigantic power shovels eating the earth in a pit already two hundred yards deep and a half mile across" (131).

Hillerman's novel is a tale of murder, betrayal, and witchery, centered on amulets made of black stone in the shape of a mole, the animal known as "people of darkness" in the Diné language. The passing of the amulets spreads radioactivity and death among a local cult suspected of witchcraft. The black stone is pitchblende, an ore of uranium.

Similar themes illuminate the writing of the poet, novelist, and essayist Leslie Marmon Silko. Silko claims an ethnic mix that represents the entire population of New Mexico, but her deepest identification lies with the place and people of Laguna Pueblo, which in the 1950s played host to the Jackpile Mine, at the time the largest open-pit uranium mine in the world (Ortiz, *Woven Stone*, 22).

The map may tell you that her home is an Indian reservation, but for the Laguna people, it is far more. It is the Pueblo equivalent of living in Eden, at least mythologically, the place where this world was first glimpsed by humankind. "Even now," Silko writes in her essay "Landscape, History, and the Pueblo Imagination," "the people at Laguna Pueblo spend the greater portion of social occasions recounting recent incidents or events which have occurred in the Laguna area. Nearly always, the discussion will precipitate the retelling of older stories about similar incidents or other stories connected with a specific place" (40). Further, she writes:

> [Since] the stories about boulders, springs, and hills are actually remnants from a ritual that retraces the creation and emergence of the Laguna Pueblo people as a culture, as the people they became, then continued use of that route creates a unique relationship between the ritual-mystic world and the actual,

Laguna Pueblo

everyday world. A journey from Paguate to Laguna down the long incline of Paguate Hill retraces the original journey from the Emergence Place, which is slightly north of the Paguate village. Thus the landscape between Paguate and Laguna takes on a deeper significance; the landscape resonates the spiritual or mythic dimension of the Pueblo world. (38)

In this spirit, Silko's treatment of witchery in her stories and novels, which depend deeply upon indigenous storytelling, brings to life the Faustian or world-destroying side of the modern myth inspired by nuclear science and history, the counterpart of the Promethean side, which plays out in the heroic depictions of the Manhattan Project in Anglo histories, novels, and films, as well as in the comic-book figure of the superhero. Like no other imaginative writer, Silko develops Oppenheimer's insight into the postnuclear human being as *destroyer of worlds*.

Her masterpiece is the novel *Ceremony*, a performance unsurpassed in the world literature emerging from the Atomic Age. If you read nothing else from the literary tour of Nuclear New Mexico, read this.

The story unfolds from the moment the protagonist Tayo is forced to carry his mortally wounded comrade and cousin Rocky through the jungle in the Bataan Death March—an atrocity in the history of World War II with special resonance for New Mexicans because so many of the state's sons died there in the drenched trudge through the Philippine jungles as prisoners of the Japanese. Those who survived were often plagued with survivor's guilt and what we now call post-traumatic stress disorder (PTSD), which is the fate of the main character in *Ceremony*.

Tayo has taken a vow to care for his cousin Rocky during the war; Rocky is a former football star and Indian success story who talked Tayo into enlisting for the armed services. Rocky ultimately dies as Tayo and another soldier struggle to carry him through the rain. In frustration and despair, Tayo curses the rain, and when he returns to New Mexico without his cousin, he finds the world in drought, the result, in his way of thinking, of the words he had carelessly pronounced in his time of struggle: "He had prayed the rain away, and for the sixth year it was dry" (13). In his indigenous worldview, where words have the power to alter reality, the curse he utters in frustration and fear is equivalent to witchery.

Words have power, as the realizations of thought. The one who created the world is called "Thought Woman" in the Pueblo pantheon: "Whatever she thinks about / appears" (1). So in the ceremonial way of thinking introduced mainly through the poems scattered throughout *Ceremony*: "You don't have anything / if you don't have the stories" (2). The world is made, and unmade, by words and thoughts, by stories.

While remaining rooted in his ethnic and regional identity, Tayo offers an image of humanity suddenly aware of, and tormented by, a newfound power. How can a modern reader understand this view of power, which hinges on an indigenous understanding of words, stories, curses, and witchery and yet is offered in English, in the modern literary form of the novel? Like the white doctors who can do nothing to heal Tayo of his "battle fatigue" and "hallucinations" but who still forbid "Indian medicine" (31), the modern reader, even a modern Indian reader (like Tayo's cousin Rocky)—educated in the scientific system, where local knowledge has been surmounted by the kind of global awareness that the world wars and the scale of destruction available in the Atomic Age render fully possible—may look upon Tayo's anxiety about the power of bad thoughts and careless words as superstitious, if not dangerously delusional. Modern psychology would say that the collapse of careful distinctions in his world is clearly the result of PTSD—the blurring of the past and present, dreams and reality (so that another story of PTSD, *Grizzly Years*, from the same period of composition but written by an Anglo, the Vietnam veteran Doug Peacock, follows a similar pattern of skipping around in time, even though it is nonfictional and not an experimental novel with roots in indigenous ceremonies). In this modern way of thinking,

Petroglyph of indigenous people in cornfield

there is no need for a literal reading of Tayo's troubles as the result of his own heedless words and thoughts in the heat of war. The distorted and tangled lines of the narrative mimic his illness.

But how different, really, is Tayo's understanding of the power of words and thoughts from that of the men who invented the atomic bomb? They too were caught in a difficult spot by their service in the war: between their vow to save the world from fascism and their commitment to the survival of the species, with the added temptation of the chance to pursue technical excellence to its highest realization. "Before there was a physical bomb, there was a virtual bomb, a bomb in the mind," writes Jonathan Schell (*Seventh Decade*, 26). Once the thought was there, the bomb was all but inevitable, fated. As Schell has noted, the "fathers" of the bomb have said as much. Robert Oppenheimer: "When you see something that is technically sweet, you go ahead and do it and you argue about what to do about it only after you have had your technical success" (quoted in Schell, *Seventh Decade*, 19). Edward Teller: "If the development is possible, it is out of our power to prevent it" (20). John von Neumann: "If it can be made, it will be made"—"a principle," says Schell, "that, if applied, might one day be a fitting epitaph for the human species" (20). Compare with Silko's figure of Thought Woman: "Whatever she thinks about / appears" (1).

The parallels between Tayo's mythic world and the world of the new atomic human, once noticed, seem to proliferate. For example, from the film *The Day after Trinity* comes a bit of lore concerning the day that the first atomic bomb was tested. It's repeated elsewhere in various versions. Somebody was taking bets on the kiloton yield of "the gadget" when some junior scientists were horrified to hear the famous physicist Enrico Fermi, a puckish Italian with a sense of humor, suggest that the explosion might destroy the entire state of New Mexico. Many years earlier, Edward Teller had raised the possibility that the bomb might incinerate the atmosphere (see Rhodes, *Making of the Atomic Bomb*). The thought was on the mind of many in the days leading up to Trinity, but any suggestion of a bet on the matter had to be a joke. It would have been a bet that the winner could never collect.

The figure of the Gambler, who thus makes an appearance in the history of the Trinity test, was well known to the indigenous peoples of the Southwest—and especially the Navajo, the neighbors who sometimes raided as enemies and sometimes traded with the Laguna people. The Gambler changes the world by his actions. The ballad "In the Land of the Navajo" by the Americana singer-songwriter Peter Rowan borrows from this myth in the tale of One-Eyed Jack the Gambler and his Indian friend Running Elk. Running Elk wagers the elements of the cosmos (the Mississippi River, Jupiter, and Mars) for a handful of turquoise stones. The game comes to its conclusion with Running Elk declaring with his dying words that the white man rules the land. The Gambler wins but becomes the white destroyer of worlds, acquisitive and aggressive beyond all bounds. He ends by casting the stones into the sky and sounding a mournful cry.

The story of the physicists' wager was probably unknown to Silko when she was writing *Ceremony*. But she definitely drew on the lore of the Gambler in a poem she included about a contest of witches, which leads to a nuclear conclusion.

Witches from all over the world gather to compete, "the way people have baseball tournaments nowadays" (123). To the event come Zuni and Navajo and Hopi witches as well as witches from across the ocean. The skinwalkers come, who wear the hides of animals and then transfigure into the animals: "fox, badger, bobcat, and wolf" (123). All the old tricks are played, cheap magic purveyed, and familiar spells cast before the showing off begins, and somebody says, "That wasn't anything, / watch this."

As the competition heats up, something utterly different emerges: a witch who has stayed in the shadows while the others show off, one who couldn't be identified by tribe or even by gender. This one says, "What I have is a story" (124). The others laugh and then grow quiet.

The witch tells of "white skin people / like the belly of a fish / covered with hair" who live in caves across the ocean. "They grow away

Petroglyph of elk, Bandelier National Monument

from the earth" and the sun and animals. "When they look, / they see only objects. / The world is a dead thing for them." They grow to fear the world because they see it as different from themselves. Then they seek to destroy what they fear. Ultimately they cross the ocean on the winds, "thousands of them in giant boats, / swarming like larva / out of a crushed anthill." Their destructive nature leads them finally to the ultimate end:

in these hills
they will find the rocks,
rocks with veins of green and yellow and black
they will lay the final pattern with these rocks
they will lay it across the world
and explode everything. (125–27)

The rocks, of course, contain the uranium mined on Navajo and Laguna land in the time of the war and just after. The ultimate pattern of self-destruction discovered by the witch's tools, the white people, is the atomic bomb.

Mount Taylor from Acoma

The story strikes fear in the hearts of the other witches, who now seem ridiculous "in their stinking animal skins, fur and feathers," the pitiable vestments of their outdated magic. They say, "Okay you win; you take the prize, / but what you said just now—it isn't so funny /. . . . Call that story back" (127–28).

But the witch just shook its head
at the others. . . .
It's already turned loose.
It's already coming.
It can't be called back. (128)

Somebody in the summer of 1945 must have voiced a similar response to the dark humor of the legendary wager made at Trinity Site, about destroying the entire state or incinerating the atmosphere: it isn't so funny; don't even say it. And then there's the comment of the physicist Freeman Dyson in his memoir *Disturbing the Universe*, a book that takes the Faustian bargain as the key myth of the Atomic Age: once the atomic bomb was invented, humanity was doomed to have it forever. Even if the stockpiles of weapons could be dismantled, destroyed, shot away into deep space, or incinerated in the sun, the idea for making the thing, the formulas and recipes, the words and thoughts, the story, the bomb in the mind, would remain. It can't be called back.

The suggestion is that nuclear science, and perhaps modern technology as a whole, is not *like* witchery; it *is* witchery. It begins by seeking power over others—perhaps others, like the Nazis and Japanese Imperialists, who deserved to be met with force, and including nonhuman enemies, like the plant and insect pests targeted by the chemical industry exposed in Rachel Carson's *Silent Spring*—but it ends by spinning out of control. What scientists and philosophers are accustomed to call "unintended consequences" or what military people call "collateral damage" or what medical people call "side effects" expand to include nearly everyone and everything. By then, it can't be called back.

The best example is the Manhattan Project itself. The original motive was to beat Hitler to the bomb. Many of the participants were Jewish émigrés who had experienced the maliciousness of Nazism firsthand. But then Hitler was defeated, and yet the work continued—the technical sweetness of the bomb, as Oppenheimer called it, proving irresistible to most of the scientists. Then once the device proved possible, it was practically fated to be used. The justification became the saving of Allied lives that would otherwise be sacrificed in an invasion of the Japanese homeland. Then came the Russians and the Cold War and the allure of the H-bomb as the ultimate weapon.

The lingering memory of the bomb, burned into cultural memory, is represented in *Ceremony* by the seeming miracle of blind people who are able to see the Trinity blast or sighted people who can't unsee it. Tayo's Laguna grandmother tells the story. Her testament follows a brief interlude that amounts to a straightforward report on uranium mining on the Cebolleta Land Grant near Laguna (which Tayo traverses in his search for his uncle's lost cattle and his quest for his own cure). The work began in 1943. At the time, nobody objected when the government cars came driving in, bringing the strangers who prospected and then mined the land: "The drought had killed off most of the cattle by then, so it didn't matter if a square mile of land was off limits, with high barbed-wire fences around it" (226). By 1945, the mine had played out and was abandoned. That was the year Grandma had her vision, which she tells to Tayo just after his return from the war:

Old Grandma told him while he was still sick and weak, lying in the darkened room. She shuffled in and sat down on the edge of his bed. "I have been thinking of something," she said. "It happened while you were gone. I had to get up, the way I do, to use the chamber pot. It was still dark; everyone else was still sleeping. But as I walked back from the kitchen to my bed there was a flash of light through the window. So big, so bright even my old clouded-up eyes could see it. It must have filled the whole southeast sky. I thought I was seeing the sun rise again, but it faded away, and by that time the dogs around here were barking. . . . Your auntie laughed at me when I told her what I saw. But later on that day, Romero came around. He said he saw it too. So bright that it blinded him for a moment; then later he could still see it flashing when he closed his eyes. . . . You know, I have never understood that thing I saw. Later on there was something about it in the newspaper. Strongest thing on this earth. Biggest explosion that ever happened. . . . Now I only wonder why, grandson. Why did they make a thing like that?" (227–28)

As Tayo knows, "Trinity Site, where they exploded the first atomic bomb, was only three hundred miles to the southeast, at White Sands. And the top secret laboratories where the bomb had been created were deep in the Jemez Mountains, only a hundred miles northeast of him now, still surrounded by high electric fences and the ponderosa pine and tawny sandrock of the Jemez mountain canyon where the shrine of the twin mountain lions had always been" (228). Situated between the point of the bomb's development and ground zero, Grandma witnessed the event that changed the world, miraculous in its way. Like some mighty god, it enabled the blind to see, if only for a moment; and it blinded the sighted people, like the neighbor Romero who saw it and never stopped seeing it.

The story recalls a recurring dream that the Utah writer Terry Tempest Williams tells in her memoir *Refuge*:

I told my father that for years, as I long as I could remember, I saw this flash of light in the desert—that this image had so permeated my being that I could not venture south without seeing it again, on the horizon, illuminating buttes and mesas.

"You did see it," he said.

"Saw what?"

"The bomb. The cloud. We were driving home from Riverside, California. You were sitting on Diane's lap. In fact, I remember the day, September 7, 1957. We had just gotten out of the service. We were driving north, past Las Vegas. It was an hour or so before dawn, when this explosion went off. I thought the oil tanker in front of us had blown up. We pulled over and suddenly, rising out of the desert floor, we saw it, clearly, this golden-stemmed cloud, the mushroom. Within a few minutes, a light ash was raining on the car."

I stared at my father.

"I thought you knew that," he said. "It was a common occurrence in the fifties."

It was at that moment that I realized the deceit I had been living under. Children growing up in the American Southwest, drinking contaminated milk from contaminated cows, even from the contaminated breasts of their mothers, my mother—members, years later, of the Clan of One-Breasted Women. (282–83)

Williams likes tribal language. And, after all, Europeans once lived in tribes as well and had their own animisms, a legacy that Williams's Mormon heritage reawakens, to some extent. The Clan of One-Breasted Women is composed of the downwinders who in the decades immediately following the flurry of testing in the Nevada desert suffered an unusually high incidence of breast cancer. Like the Cebolleta people who scavenged the old mine site, and the Navajos who used discarded sand from the uranium mines for adobe to build homes (see Pasternak, *Yellow Dirt*), the witnesses to the testing, in the light rain of ash, became unwitting participants in the great experiment carried out by the US government. Williams's language connects the Clan of One-Breasted Women to the Navajo and Laguna Pueblo people, the Spanish of the Cebolleta Land Grant, and the ranchers of the Tularosa Basin, who grew up with the effects of uranium mining and bomb testing written into their genetic legacy. The borders of the child's dream and her reality, like those of the soldier suffering from PTSD, dissolve. They become sites on the shadow of the shadow tour.

Even closer to Grandma's story, geographically and historically (if not in spirit), are similar accounts given by witnesses interviewed in Joe Else's documentary film *The Day after Trinity* and reported by Paul Boyer in his history *By the Bomb's Early Light: American Thought and Culture at the Dawn of the Atomic Age.* "Newspaper stories told of Georgia Green," for example, "a blind girl in Albuquerque, 120 miles from [Trinity Site], who at the moment of the detonation had cried out, 'What was that?'" (Boyer, *By the Bomb's Early Light*, 6). The story became part of the local lore in New Mexico. Silko likely knew it well and brought it into her novel.

In one of the prose/poetry performances collected in *Woven Stone* and titled "Our Homeland, a National Sacrifice Area" (337), Simon Ortiz shows how the Trinity blast became the benchmark for other incidents involving the shifting and overpowering of seemingly eternal natural events, like sunrise:

> In 1966, when the El Paso Natural Gas Company pipeline ruptured at Deechuna and shot exploding flames five hundred feet into the sky, old man Sharrowka said, "I had gotten up quite early, put wood in the stove, and I felt the light, but I knew it was not going to be sunrise yet. And then I looked, and the light was in the wrong place." And my father remembered an earlier time, "I got up that morning because the light was strange. It could not be the sun I thought to myself, and when I looked the light was too far to the south. It shimmered and faded, and it did not settle." I was only a few years old when the false dawn happened in 1945, rising out of the southeastern New Mexican plains. Some people recall that strange dawn as a tremor of light they could feel passing through them. (352)

The false dawn in 1945 came from the explosion at Trinity, of course. In shadow country, it foretold other explosions and signaled an array of changes that followed the unleashing of technology on a grand scale, the seeming competition of humanity with nature.

Silko's *Ceremony* is not the only book from the Cold War with witchery

Acoma
Pueblo
corn

on the mind. You don't have to read very far into the history of environmental literature to find the theme, again connected loosely with atomic weaponry. Books like Rachel Carson's *Silent Spring* (1962) and Paul Ehrlich's *Population Bomb* (1968), at the historical onset of environmentalism as we know it today, borrowed imagery from the bomb culture of the Cold War to warn of a dire crisis in the natural environment. Carson also draws on the language of witchcraft in her exposé of the chemical pesticide industry. She speaks of spells, brews, and rains of death (see Killingsworth and Palmer, *Ecospeak*, 67–69). She concludes her famous preface "A Fable for Tomorrow" by declaring that "no witchcraft, no enemy action had silenced the rebirth of new life in this stricken world"—the ruined landscape of the formerly pastoral America—"the people had done it to themselves" (14). In drawing together the language of nuclear apocalypse, witchcraft, and the ruined land, Carson's vision anticipates Silko's *Ceremony* (see Killingsworth and Palmer, "Millennial Ecology"; Glotfelty, "Cold War"; Lutts, "Chemical Fallout"; Waddell, *"And No Birds Sing"*).

The big difference is that while Silko seems seriously to blame witchery ("the destroyers") more than any other clearly identified social group or political ideology for the woes of atomic weaponry, modern war, racial injustice, and environmental destruction, Carson ultimately discards witchcraft as a mere metaphor, a vehicle for her warning, while strongly hinting that science has made possible the kind of power that witches of olden times and fairy tales could not have imagined in their most vicious dreams of absolute power over others. A similar way of thinking appears in the interpretation of the Manhattan Project as a Faustian bargain or Promethean curse (see Dyson, *Disturbing the Universe*; Bird and Sherwin, *American Prometheus*).

Another difference is that Carson's "Fable for Tomorrow" does a very modern and scientific thing—selecting details from a variety of sites to create a composite or hypothetical town "in the heart of America"—while Silko's story stays grounded in the tribal lands of her people, in the nuclearized landscape of New Mexico. It is a place where witchcraft has been taken very seriously. The local Hispanic people, who share with Indians and Anglos in the heralded tricultural diversity of the state, brought their own version of witchcraft from the Old World, and their beliefs mingled with those of the indigenous peoples of the region (see Simmons, *Witchcraft in the Southwest*). Their version is on display in the memorable 1972 novel *Bless Me, Ultima*, by Rudolfo Anaya, a native of Santa Rosa and longtime professor of creative writing at the University of New Mexico. The novel is clearly a product of postwar changes and the Cold War mood, complete with reflections on the experiences of veterans returning from World War II—in this case, the dissatisfaction felt by the narrator's older brothers, who have "seen the world" and, like Tayo's Laguna friends in Silko's novel, can no longer feel at ease in the simplicity of the rural homeplace. The bomb is not blamed outright, but in pitting the forces of the *curandera* against those of dark witchery, Anaya's novel resonates with Carson's depiction of good science versus evil science. It captures the ambivalence that readers of the era would have felt toward the newfound powers of the human race. Is Ultima a witch or a healer, a demon or a savior? Is Oppenheimer a Faust or a Prometheus, a destroyer or a savior of humanity?

The question remains, though, of what to make of witchery today. Many sociologists and anthropologists, like the specialist on New Mexican witchcraft Clyde Kluckhohn, would tell you to take a "functional" approach to the problem. Look for motives, both cultural and personal, in calling somebody a witch. Historically, witch hunters have targeted elderly (and especially bitter) members of the community, hormone-infused adolescents, unruly women, and troublesome eccentrics. The function of this kind of witch hunting is to maintain social order or to secure power for a particular social group (priests, patriarchs, politicians, and the like). Another purpose is to make people behave. An accusation of witchcraft amounts to a dramatic way of saying that something or someone is wrong, bad, and socially unacceptable.

The functional approach may help in a limited way to make sense

Acoma Pueblo on the distant mesa

of characters like Tayo's fellow veteran Emo in *Ceremony* or Ultima's foes in Anaya's novel. They serve as object lessons for what happens to people who crave power over others and fail to take care of their friends and family. But in the fable of the witches' contest, Silko goes well beyond social science. Her treatment of witchery becomes cosmic and mythological. She not only dramatizes the current predicament of humankind with reference to the old myths, but reasserts the power and presence of mythology. While not denying the allure of science and technology, she offers reasons to resist those modern sources of power and seek knowledge in the traditional domains of the poet, the storyteller, and the shaman.

Tayo becomes a figure of everyman, left to sort out the legacy and live a life defined by the appeal and danger of witchcraft's power. Once the bomb was exploded at Trinity, he muses, "there was no end to it; it knew no boundaries; and he had arrived at the point of convergence where the fate of all living things, and even the earth had been laid" (Silko, *Ceremony*, 228). The whole business ironically unites human beings even as it gives them the power to kill each other once and for all: "From that time on, human beings were one clan again, united by the fate the destroyers planned for all of them, for all living things; united by a circle of death that devoured people in cities twelve thousand miles away, victims who had never known these mesas, who had never seen the delicate colors of these rocks which boiled up their slaughter" (228).

Parting Thoughts: Tour, Quest, Pilgrimage

The literature of Nuclear New Mexico suggests two alternatives to the concept of the tour: the quest and the pilgrimage. The quest is a key figure of epic literature. We see it at work in the searching journeys of demigods and superheroes, as well as in Tayo's search for a cure and new way of being in *Ceremony*. The Manhattan Project was a quest to attain the bomb before the Nazis, to unveil the secret of the atom. The nuclear tourist is also on a quest, in search of entertainment, understanding, and enlightenment.

But the pilgrimage, as your tour guides have already hinted, is perhaps a better alternative for the imaginative traveler in Nuclear New Mexico. You go to a desert land—not unlike the traditional sites of many classic pilgrimages, the Holy Land for Jews and Christians, Mecca for Muslims—seeking the traces and places of gods and giants that walked the earth and left their relics. The pilgrim seeks their power and reflects on where it has gone. You go to be healed or enlightened, to commemorate and contemplate, to transcend the ordinary state of the touring consumer. The ecotourist and the nuclear tourist meet at the point of pilgrimage. They go with the hope of renewing the tired spirit of modern life, to reenter the flow of history (both natural and human), to find a path leading beyond daily devastation and eventual extinction.

Power attracts the pilgrim: "Pilgrimages . . . are associated with human perceptions of the extraordinary and with specific locales and buildings that are believed to contain powers that transcend the everyday nature of the world" (Reader, *Pilgrimage*, 27). You cross the state of New Mexico in search of the god species, its signs, its portents, the meaning it imparts.

You are greeted with fences and secrecy—mysteries—at every turn. Government secrecy is hailed as necessary for security in a world of espionage and terrorism and then decried for driving a wedge be-

Fenced

tween the people and the government. Modern governments impart information, and they keep secrets—just like everybody else. What is revealed is celebrated or feared; what is concealed spurs the imagination.

The fence becomes the symbol of how secrecy encroaches on history and public information. The nuclear tourist stands at the fence and wonders.

.

Bibliography

Abbey, Edward. *Desert Solitaire: A Season in the Wilderness*. New York: Ballantine, 1968.

——. *Down the River*. New York: Plume, 1991.

——. *Fire on the Mountain*. With an introduction by Gerald Haslam. 1962. Reprint, Albuquerque: University of New Mexico Press, 1978.

——. *The Fool's Progress*. New York: Holt, 1988.

——. *The Monkey Wrench Gang*. New York: Avon, 1975.

Albrecht, Glenn. "Solastalgia, a New Concept in Human Health and Identity." *PAN: Philosophy Activism Nature* 3 (2005): 41–55. Accessed June 13, 2017. http://search.informit.com.au/documentSummary;dn=897723015186456;res=IELHSS.

Anaya, Rudolfo A. *Bless Me, Ultima*. Berkeley, CA: TQS Publications, 1972.

Awiakta, Marilou. *Abiding Appalachia: Where Mountain and Atom Meet*. Memphis, TN: St. Luke's, 1990.

Barnhill, David Landis, ed. *At Home on the Earth: Becoming Native to Our Place; A Multicultural Anthology*. Berkeley: University of California Press, 1999.

Bird, Kai, and Martin J. Sherwin. *American Prometheus: The Triumph and Tragedy of J. Robert Oppenheimer*. New York: Knopf, 2005.

Bogost, Ian. *Alien Phenomenology, or What It's Like to Be a Thing*. Minneapolis: University of Minnesota Press, 2012.

Boyer, Paul. *By the Bomb's Early Light: American Thought and Culture at the Dawn of the Atomic Age*. 1985. Reprint, Chapel Hill: University of North Carolina Press, 1994.

Brugge, Doug, Timothy Benally, and Esther Yazzie-Lewis, eds. *The Navajo People and Uranium Mining*. With a foreword by Stewart L. Udall. Albuquerque: University of New Mexico Press, 2006.

Brugge, Doug, Jamie L. deLemos, and Cat Bul. "The Sequoyah Corporation Fuels Release and the Church Rock Spill: Unpublicized Nuclear Releases in American Indian Communities." *American Journal of Public Health* 97, no. 9 (2007): 1595–600.

Cahalan, James M. *Edward Abbey: A Life*. Tucson: University of Arizona Press, 2003.

Caldwell, Joseph. Interview by author. February 22, 2015.

Carson, Rachel. *Silent Spring*. New York: Fawcett Crest, 1962.

Clausing, Jeri. "Leaks, Accidents Shut Nuclear Dump." *Houston Chronicle*, February 2014. www.houstonchronicle.com.

Craig, Vincent. *Muttonman* comic strip. *Navajo Times*, February 12, February 19, February 26, June 25, 1981; March 12, August 25, September 3, 1992.

DeLillo, Don. *Underworld*. New York: Simon and Schuster, 1997.

Del Mauro, Diana. "Vincent Craig's Secrets to a Happy Life." *Navajo Times*, May 20, 2010.

Dyson, Freeman. *Disturbing the Universe*. New York: Basic, 1979.

Ehrlich, Paul R. *The Population Bomb*. 1968. Reprint, San Francisco: Sierra Club, 1969.

Eichstaedt, Peter H. *If You Poison Us: Uranium and Native Americans*. Santa Fe: Red Crane, 1994.

Eliot, T. S. *The Wasteland: Norton Critical Edition*. Edited by Michael North. New York: Norton, 2001.

Else, Jon. *The Day after Trinity: J. Robert Oppenheimer and the Atomic Bomb*. Chatsworth, CA: Image Entertainment, 1980. DVD.

"Experience Overview." Spaceport America Tour. Accessed October 11, 2017. http://spaceportamericatour.com/.

Fetter-Vorm, Jonathan. *Trinity: A Graphic History of the First Atomic Bomb*. New York: Hill and Wang, 2012.

Ford, Kenneth W. *Building the H Bomb: A Personal History*. Singapore: World Scientific, 2015.

"Gasbuggy Nuclear Test Site, New Mexico." Center for Land Use Interpretation. Accessed October 16, 2017. http://clui.org/ludb/site/gasbuggy-nuclear-test-site.

Glotfelty, Cheryll. "Cold War, *Silent Spring*: The Trope of War in Modern Environmentalism." In *"And No Birds Sing": The Rhetoric of Rachel Carson*, edited by Craig Waddell, 157–73. Carbondale: Southern Illinois University Press, 2000.

Greenwood, Phaedra. Interview by author. March 14, 2016. Taos, NM.

Harden, Blaine. "Deep in Carlsbad Cave, Hungry Tourists Prevail." *New York Times*, April 14, 2002. Accessed October 15, 2017. http://www.nytimes.com/2002/04/14/us/deep-in-carlsbad-cave-hungry-tourists-prevail.html.

Hayes, Rose O. 2015. *Politics Trumps Nuclear Science: America's Radioactive Waste Dilemma, a Social Scientist's Perspective*. Self-published, 2014. Kindle.

Hillerman, Anne. *Rock with Wings*. New York: HarperCollins, 2015. Kindle.

Hillerman, Tony. *People of Darkness*. New York: Harper, 1980.

Hodge, Nathan, and Sharon Weinberger. *A Nuclear Family Vacation: Travels in the World of Atomic Weaponry*. New York: Bloomsbury, 2011. Kindle.

Horgan, Paul. *Great River: The Rio Grande in North American History*. Middletown, CT: Wesleyan University Press, 1984.

Howe, Linda Moulton. *Alien Harvest: Further Evidence Linking Human Abductions and Animal Mutilations to Alien Life Forms*. Further Evidence Special Limited Edition. With a foreword by Jacque Vallee. Self-published, 1989.

"How Volcanoes Influence Climate." UCAR Center for Science Education. Accessed October 4, 2017. http://scied.ucar.edu/shortcontent/how-volcanoes-influence-climate.

Hunner, Jon. "Reinventing Los Alamos: Code Switching and Suburbia in America's Atomic City." In *Atomic Culture: How We Learned to Stop Worrying and Love the Bomb*, edited by Scott C. Zeman and Michael A. Amundson, 33–48. Boulder: University Press of Colorado, 2004.

Johnson, Robert R. *Romancing the Atom: Nuclear Infatuation from the Radium Girls to Fukushima*. Santa Barbara, CA: Praeger, 2013.

"Jumbo." Trinity Atomic Web Site. US Department of Energy, National Atomic Museum, Albuquerque, NM. 2017. Accessed September 13, 2017. http://www.abomb1.org/trinity/trinity2.html.

Kanon, Joseph. *Los Alamos*. New York: Broadway, 1997.

Killingsworth, M. Jimmie. *Facing It: Epiphany and Apocalypse in the New Nature*. College Station: Texas A&M University Press, 2014.

Killingsworth, M. Jimmie, and Jacqueline S. Palmer. *Ecospeak: Rhetoric and Environmental Politics in America*. Carbondale: Southern Illinois University Press, 1992.

——. "Millennial Ecology: The Apocalyptic Narrative from Silent Spring to Global Warming." In *Green Culture: Environmental Rhetoric in Contemporary America*, edited by Carl G. Herndl and Stuart C. Brown, 21–45. Madison: University of Wisconsin Press, 1996.

"Kirtland AFB History." US Air Force, Kirtland Air Force Base. March 27, 2013. Accessed October 2017. http://www.kirtland.af.mil/About-Us/Fact-Sheets/Display/Article/825960/kirtland-afb-history/.

"Kirtland Air Force Base Welcome: Mission and Major Organizations." US Air Force, Kirtland Air Force Base. Accessed October 2017. http://www.kirtland.af.mil/Home/Welcome/.

Kluckhohn, Clyde. *Navaho Witchcraft*. 1944. Reprint, Boston: Beacon, 1963.

Kosek, Jake. *Understories: The Political Life of Forests in Northern New Mexico*. Durham, NC: Duke University Press, 2006.

Kristofic, Jim. *Navajos Wear Nikes: A Reservation Life*. Albuquerque: University of New Mexico Press, 2011.

Kuletz, Valerie L. *The Tainted Desert: Environmental and Social Ruin in the American West*. New York: Routledge, 1998.

Leopold, Aldo. *A Sand County Almanac, and Sketches Here and There*. New York: Oxford University Press, 1989.

Locke, Raymond Friday. *The Book of the Navajo*. 5th ed. Los Angeles: Mankind, 1992.

"Los Alamos National Laboratory." US Department of Energy, National Nuclear Security Administration. 2016. Accessed October 2017. http://www.lanl.gov.

Lutts, Ralph H. "Chemical Fallout: *Silent Spring*, Radioactive Fallout, and the Environmental Movement." In *"And No Birds Sing": The Rhetoric of Rachel Carson*, edited by Craig Waddell, 17–41. Carbondale: Southern Illinois University Press, 2000.

Lynas, Mark. *The God Species: Saving the Planet in the Age of Humans*. Washington, DC: National Geographic, 2011.

McPhee, John. *The Curve of Binding Energy*. New York: Ballantine, 1974.

Memmott, Mark. "A Los Alamos Landmark, the 'Black Hole,' Is About to Disappear." *The Two-Way: Breaking News from NPR*. September 17, 2012. http://www.npr.org/blogs/thetwo-way/2012/09/17/161271167/a-los-alamos-landmark-the-black-hole-is-about-to-disappear.

Miller, Jimmy. Interview by author. October 20, 2017.

Monk, Ray. *Robert Oppenheimer: A Life inside the Center*. New York: Doubleday, 2012.

Moore, Alan, and Dave Gibbons. *Watchmen*. New York: DC Comics, 1987.

Morgan, Eric L. "Regional Communication and Sense of Place Surrounding the Waste Isolation Pilot Plant." In *Nuclear Legacies: Communication, Controversies, and the U.S. Weapons Complex*, edited by Bryan C. Taylor, William J. Kinsella, Stephen P. Depoe, and Maribeth S. Metzler, 109–32. Lanham, MD: Rowman and Littlefield, 2007.

Ortiz, Simon J. *Woven Stone*. Tucson: University of Arizona Press, 1992.

Pasternak, Judy. *Yellow Dirt: An American Story of a Poisoned Land and a People Betrayed*. New York: Free Press, 2010.

Peacock, Doug. *Grizzly Years*. New York: Holt, 1990.

Pezzullo, Phaedra C. *Toxic Tourism: Rhetorics of Pollution, Travel, and Environmental Justice*. 2nd ed. Tuscaloosa: University of Alabama Press, 2014. Kindle.

Reader, Ian. *Pilgrimage: A Very Short Introduction*. Oxford: Oxford University Press, 2015.

Rekow, Lea. "Monument Valley, AZ. Mexican Hat UMTRA Site." Ex-Tract: Mineral Extraction and Cultural Ecology on the Colorado Plateau. 2013. Accessed May 2016. http://www.learekow.com/extract/content/mexicanhat.php.

Rhodes, Richard. *Dark Sun: The Making of the Hydrogen Bomb*. New York: Simon and Schuster, 1996.

———. *The Making of the Atomic Bomb*. New York: Simon and Schuster, 1986.

Robinson, William Paul. "Uranium Production and Its Effects on Navajo Communities along the Rio Puerco in Western New Mexico." In *Proceedings of the Michigan Conference on Race and the Incidence of Environmental Hazards*, edited by Bunyan Bryant and Paul Mohai, 175–86. Ann Arbor: University of Michigan School of Natural Resources, 1990.

"Rocket Fever!" Spaceport America. June 29, 2017. Accessed October 11, 2017. https://spaceportamerica.com/rocket-fever-was-everywhere-last-week-at-spaceport-america-in-new-mexico/.

Rogers, Simon. "Nuclear Power Plant Accidents: Listed and Ranked Since 1952." *The Guardian*, January 13, 2015. Accessed October 2017. http://www.theguardian.com/news/datablog/2011/mar/14/nuclear-power-plant-accidents-list-rank#data.

"Sandia National Laboratories: History." 2017. Accessed October 9, 2017. http://www.sandia.gov/about/history/index.html.

"Sandia National Laboratories: Mission." 2017. Accessed October 9, 2017. http://www.sandia.gov/about/mission/index.html.

Scarry, Elaine. *Thermonuclear Monarchy: Choosing between Democracy and Doom*. New York: Norton, 2014. Kindle.

Schell, Jonathan. *The Fate of the Earth*. New York: Knopf, 1982.

———. *The Seventh Decade: The New Shape of Nuclear Danger*. New York: Holt, 2007.

Schlosser, Eric. *Command and Control: Nuclear Weapons, the Damascus Accident, and the Illusion of Safety.* New York: Penguin, 2013.

Shuey, Chris. Interview by author. August 2012. Albuquerque, NM.

Silko, Leslie Marmon. *Ceremony.* With an introduction by Larry McMurtry and a new preface by L. M. Silko. 1977. Reprint, New York: Penguin, 2006.

———. "Landscape, History, and the Pueblo Imagination." In *At Home on the Earth: Becoming Native to Our Place; A Multicultural Anthology,* edited by David Landis Barnhill, 30–50. Berkeley: University of California Press, 1999.

Simmons, Marc. *Witchcraft in the Southwest.* 1974. Reprint, Lincoln: University of Nebraska Press, 1980.

Smith, Martin Cruz. *Stallion Gate.* New York: Random House, 1986.

SRIC (Southwest Research and Information Center). "Church Rock Uranium Mill Tailings Spill and Uranium Legacy Remembrance and Action Day." SRIC Information Sheet. December 7, 2009.

Szasz, Ferenc Morton. *Atomic Comics: Cartoonists Confront the Nuclear World.* Reno: University of Nevada Press, 2012.

———. *The Day the Sun Rose Twice: The Story of the Trinity Site Nuclear Explosion, July 16, 1945.* Albuquerque: University of New Mexico Press, 1984.

Taylor, Bryan C., William J. Kinsella, Stephen P. Depoe, and Maribeth S. Metzler, eds. *Nuclear Legacies: Communication, Controversies, and the U.S. Weapons Complex.* Lanham, MD: Rowman and Littlefield, 2007.

Udall, Stewart L. *The Myths of August: A Personal Explanation of Our Tragic Cold War Affair with the Atom.* 1994. Reprint, New Brunswick, NJ: Rutgers University Press, 1998.

Valdez, Greg. *Dulce Base: The Truth and Evidence from the Case Files of Gabe Valdez.* Albuquerque: Levi-Cash, 2013.

Van Wyck, Peter C. "American Monument: The Waste Isolation Pilot Plant." In *Atomic Culture: How We Learned to Stop Worrying and Love the Bomb,* edited by Scott C. Zeman and Michael A. Amundson, 149–72. Boulder: University of Colorado Press.

Waddell, Craig, ed. *"And No Birds Sing": The Rhetoric of Rachel Carson.* Carbondale: Southern Illinois University Press, 2000.

Weigle, Marta, and Peter White. *The Lore of New Mexico.* Albuquerque: University of New Mexico Press, 1988.

Weinstein, Simcha. *Up, Up, and Oy Vey! How Jewish History, Culture, and Values Shaped the Comic Book Superheroes.* Baltimore: Leviathan, 2006.

Williams, Terry Tempest. *Refuge: An Unnatural History of Family and Place.* New York: Vintage, 1991.

YuccaMountain.org. Eureka County, Nevada—Nuclear Waste Office. Current Program News. Accessed October 17, 2017. www.yuccamountain.org.

Zeman, Scott C., and Michael A. Amundson, eds. 2004. *Atomic Culture: How We Learned to Stop Worrying and Love the Bomb.* Boulder: University of Colorado Press.

Index

Abbey, Edward, 4, 96
Abert's squirrel, 70
Abiding Appalachia: Where Mountain and Atom Meet, 55
Acoma Pueblo, NM, 108–10, 178–79, 185
Aiken, SC, 43
Alamogordo, NM, xi, 38–39, 152
Albrecht, Glenn, 49
Albuquerque Isotopes, 79
Albuquerque, NM, 12, 21, 52, 78–93, 163
Alien Harvest: Further Evidence Linking Human Abductions and Animal Mutilations to Alien Life Forms, 148
Alien Phenomenology, Or What It's Like to Be a Thing, 83
aliens, 54, 145–46, 148, 150, 152–55, 157
americium, 43
Amigos Bravos, 57, 103
Inconvenient Truth, An, 35
Anaconda Corporation, 110, 170
Anaya, Rudolfo, 187, 189
Anchor Ranch, 65
Apache Canyon Trading Post, 45
Archuleta, Mount, 148
Artesia, NM, 39, 44, 142
Atomic Age/Era, 1, 4, 6, 7, 8, 10, 12, 19, 23, 37, 41, 44, 63, 76, 79, 89, 106, 134, 172–73, 180, 184
atomic banality, 166
Atomic City, 56, 60, 64–65
Atomic Comics, 162, 166–68
Atomic Culture: How We Learned to Stop Worrying and Love the Bomb, 90
Atomic Ed. *See* Grothus, Ed
Atomic Energy Commission, 144
Atomic Kid, The, 90
Atomic Man, 166–67
Atomic Mouse, 164

Atomic Rabbit, 163
Aztec, NM, 107, 142, 145

B-29 Superfortress, 79, 91–92
Bandelier National Monument, 1, 65–78, 177
Barefoot Gen, 164
Bataan Death March, 86, 172
Bathtub Row, 60–61, 63
Becquerel, Henri, 9
Begay, Fred, 55
Bells of Coronado, 90
Benally, Harry, 133
Bert the Turtle, 86
Bhagavad Gita, 8
Billy the Kid, 156
Bingham, NM, 21
birth defects, 132
Black Hole Surplus, 62–65
Blanchard Mine, 21
Bless Me, Ultima, 187
Bloomfield, NM, 142
Bosque del Apache National Wildlife Refuge, 1, 26–37
Bosque Redondo, 130
Bradbury Science Museum, 55–58, 60, 63–65, 84–86, 101, 103
Breaking Bad, 78
Buckhorn Tavern, 26
Bureau of Indian Affairs, 162
Bureau of Land Management, 69
By the Bomb's Early Light: American Thought and Culture at the Dawn of the Atomic Age, 184

cancer, 10, 36, 54, 103–4, 107, 131, 162, 183
Canyon de Chelly, NM, 123–25
Captain Marvel Battles the Dread Nuclear War, 164
Carlsbad, NM, 6, 39–49, 79, 88, 101
Carlsbad Caverns, 39, 44–49, 88
Carson, Kit, 130

Carson National Forest, 143, 145
Carson, Rachel, 180, 186–87
cattle mutilations, 145–46, 148
Center for Disease Control, 120
Ceremony, 4, 172–76, 181, 184, 186, 189–90
Chaco Canyon, NM, 5, 104
Chaucer, 12
Chavez, Frank, 26
Chernobyl, Soviet Union, 58, 111
Church Rock, NM, 58, 106, 115–21, 124, 162–63
Cibola National Forest, 95
Civil Defense, 86–87, 99
Clean Air Act of 1963, 143
Clovis, NM, 5
Code Talkers, 133, 162
Cold War, 4–6, 34, 38, 40, 43–44, 49, 54, 56, 63, 65, 87–91, 101, 103, 106, 110–11, 131, 137, 153, 155, 168, 181, 184, 186–87
Colgate, Sterling, 60
collared lizard, 157, 160
Cowboys and Aliens, 155
Craig, Vincent, 162–63
Crimson Tide, 91
Cuban Missile Crisis, 90–91

Dagwood Splits the Atom, 164
Day after Trinity, The, 175, 184
DeLillo, Don, 6, 42
Department of Energy, 40, 44, 88, 103, 137
Depp, Johnny, 133
Diné Bikéyah, 55, 103–4, 109, 119, 124, 128, 130, 133–34, 137, 142–43, 169–70
Disturbing the Universe, 180, 186
Doctorow, E. L., v, 168
DOE. *See* Department of Energy
Donne, John, 9
Dr. Manhattan, 167–68
Dr. Strangelove, 21, 89

Dulce, NM, 107, 143–50
Dulce Base: The Truth and Evidence from the Case Files of Gabe Valdez, 146
Dyson, Freeman, 180, 186

Ehrlich, Paul, 186
Eiger Sanction, The, 133
Einstein, Albert, 85, 89, 154
einsteinium, 84
Eisenhower, Dwight D., 134–35
El Paso Natural Gas Company, 144, 184
Eliot, T.S., 12
Elugelab, Marshall Islands, 9
environmentalism, 3–4, 186
Española, NM, 52, 64

Fail-Safe, 91
Farmington, NM, 142
Fat Man, 55, 79, 93
Fate of the Earth, The, 5, 34
Fermi, Enrico, 175
fiestaware, 58
Fonda, Henry, 134
Ford, John, 128–29, 133–34
Ford, Kenneth, 9, 60
Four Corners, 96, 103–4, 106–7, 122–42, 169
Four Corners Generating Station, 142–43
Four Corners Monument, 62
fracking, 144
Fruitland, NM, 142–43
Ft. Sumner, NM, 130
Fukushima, Japan, 58, 89
Fuller Lodge, 52, 59–61

gadget, the, 6, 8, 11, 19, 86, 175
Gallup, NM, 115, 119, 124
Game of Thrones, 12
Geiger counter, 19, 21, 63, 112, 133
Gen of Hiroshima, 164
Gibbons, Dave, v
global warming, 35–36, 100
God species, 1, 9, 190
Goldwater, Barry, 134
Gore, Al, 35
Gorman, R.C., 124
Goulding Museum, 127

Goulding, Harry, 124, 128–35
Grants, NM, 44, 49, 50, 51, 75
Grey, Zane, 133
Grizzly Years, 173
Grothus, Ed, 63–64
Groves, Leslie, 3, 9, 21, 52, 60, 86

Halchita, UT, 136–37, 139
Hanford, WA, 3, 43
Heidegger, Martin, 85
Heisenberg, Werner, 85
Hesperus, Mt., 143
Hillerman, Anne, 142
Hillerman, Tony, 142, 169–70
Hiroshima, Japan, xi, 4, 15, 87, 90, 93, 99, 103. 164
Hobbs, NM, 44
Hondo River, 156
Hopi, 124, 176
Hulk, the, 167–69
hydrogen bomb, 4, 9, 99–100, 110

"In the Land of the Navajo," 176
In Plain Sight, 78
International Space Hall of Fame, 38
Invasion of the Body Snatchers, 155
Iron Curtain, 5
Iron Man, 168–69

Jackpile Mine, 170
Jemez Mountains, 98, 182
Jicarilla Apache, 107, 143
Jones, Sam, 25
Jornada del Muerto, 26, 38
Jumbo, 8, 16–17, 19

Kerr-McGee Nuclear Fuels, 110, 170
Kirtland, NM, 142
Kirtland Air Force Base, 79, 82, 84, 99–100

Ladron Peak, 99
Laguna Pueblo, NM, 109, 170–72, 176–77, 181, 187
LANL. *See* Los Alamos National Laboratories
Las Cruces, NM, 26, 37
Lawrence Radiation Laboratory, 144
Lawrence, Ernest, 60, 86
Lee, Ang, 167, 169

Lee, Stan, 167
leetso, 130, 133
Leopold, Aldo, 4
Lincoln, NM, 156
Little Boy, 55, 79, 93
Llano Estacado, 98
Lone Ranger, The, 133
Lord of the Rings, The, 12
Los Alamos, NM, xi, 1, 3–4, 6, 15, 17, 43, 49–65, 67, 79, 84–88, 98, 100–101, 103, 110, 113, 131, 146, 154, 169
Los Alamos Historical Museum, 55, 58, 60, 113
Los Alamos National Laboratories, 50, 52–56, 76, 78, 82, 84
Los Alamos Ranch School, 58–59, 60, 64–65
Los Lunas, NM, 99
Lovington, NM, 44

Magdalena Mountains, 10, 96, 99
Making of the Atomic Bomb, The, 8–9, 155, 175
Manhattan (television series), 101
Manhattan Project, xi, 3, 6, 8, 10, 60, 63, 65, 79, 85–86, 106, 154–55, 172, 181, 186, 190
Manhattan Project National Historic Park, 63
Mann, Adam, 166, 168
Manzano Mountains, 79, 82–83, 96–97
Martian Chronicles, 62
Martin, George R. R., 12
Martinez, Paddy, 110, 112
McDonald Ranch, 13, 19
McPhee, John, 85, 111
Mescalero Apaches, 156
Mexican Hat Rock, 141
Mexican Hat Uranium Mill Tailings Remedial Site, 137, 139
Milagro Beanfield War, The, 4
Monument Valley, UT, 124–37, 142
Moore, Alan, v, 167
Muench, Josef, 133
Muir, John, 4
Muttonman, 162–64
Mutual Assured Destruction, 5, 87

Nagasaki, Japan, xi, 15, 36, 90, 93, 103
National Center for Atmospheric Research, 10
National Museum of Nuclear Science and History, 21, 84–93, 99, 163, 165
National Science Foundation, 56
Navajo (Diné), 55, 96, 103–4, 109–10, 115, 119–21, 124, 128, 130–34, 136–37, 142–43, 162–64, 169, 176–77, 183
Navajo Generating Station, 143
Navajo Times, xiii, 162
Navajo Tribal Park, 124, 134, 136
Neumann, John von, 175
New Mexico Institute of Mining and Technology, 15, 29, 60
New Mexico Mining Museum, 112–13
New Mexico Museum of Space History, 38
New Mexico Tech. *See* New Mexico Institute of Mining and Technology
Nichols, John, 4
NM 599, 52
nostalgia, 44, 49, 88–91, 101, 132, 156
Nuclear Family Vacation: Travels in the World of Atomic Weaponry, A, 84, 101

Oak Ridge, TN, 3, 43, 55
On The Beach, 91
Oppenheimer, Frank, 8, 57
Oppenheimer, Robert, 1, 3, 6, 8–10, 21, 26, 50, 52, 60–61, 63, 85–86, 166, 172, 181, 187
Ortiz, Simon, 110–11, 169–70
Oscura Mountains, 9, 25, 96, 156
Owl Bar, 26, 28–29

Paguate, NM, 172
Painted Cave, 74
Painted Desert, 120
Paiute, 42
Pajarito Plateau, 52, 62, 65
Pasternak, Judy, 103–4, 120, 129–31, 133–35, 183
Peacock, Doug, 173
Pecos, NM, 3
Pecos River, 150
People of Darkness, 169–70

Permian Basin, 40
Pickens, Slim, 21
pitchblende, 170
plutonium, 8, 43, 91, 103
Population Bomb, 186
potash, 44
Project Gasbuggy, 144–45
Project Plowshare, 144
Prometheus, v, 9, 187
Pueblo Revolt, 26

radon, 137
Rattlesnake Sam. *See* Jones, Sam
Red Deuce Mine, 170
Redford, Robert, 4
Refuge, 182
Rhodes, Richard, 8–9, 21, 154–55, 165, 175
Richardson, Bill, 4
Rio Grande Rift, 25–26
Rio Grande River, 10, 29
Rio Grande Valley, 83
Rio Puerco, 119–21, 124, 162–63
Roswell, 153
Roswell, NM, 88, 107, 150–57
Roswell UFO Museum, 152
Rotblat, Sir Joseph, 64
Rowan, Peter, 176
Russians Are Coming, the Russians Are Coming, The, 91

Sacramento Mountains, 156
San Antonio, NM, 26
San Francisco Peaks, 143
San Juan Basin, 145
San Juan Mountains, 143
San Juan River, 124, 137
San Mateo Mountains, 10
sandhill cranes, 29, 33
Sandia Mountains, 83–84, 96
Sandia National Laboratories, 79–83, 101, 110
Sandia Crest/Peak, 81, 93–100
Santa Fe, NM, 12, 49, 52, 64, 74, 79, 93, 101
Santa Rosa, NM, 187
Scarry, Elaine, 87, 155
Schell, Jonathan, 5, 34–36, 39, 175
School of Mines. *See* New Mexico Institute of Mining and Technology

"Shallow Depression, A," 15, 19
Ship Rock, 142–43
Shiprock, NM, 142
Shoshone, 42
Shroud of Turin, 54
Shuey, Chris, 104, 106, 119–20
Sierra Blanca, 34, 96, 99, 156
Silent Spring, 180, 186
Silko, Leslie Marmon, 4, 170, 172, 175–76, 184, 186–87, 189
Silkwood, 91, 121
skinwalkers, 176
Sky City. *See* Acoma
Smith, Will T., 133
snow geese, 29, 33
Socorro, NM, 15, 25–26, 37, 60, 96
Southwest Research and Information Center, 104
Soviet Union, 5, 43, 49, 87–88, 99, 110–11
Space Age, xii, 37–38
Spaceport America, NM, 37
Spiderman, 162–63, 167–68
Stagecoach, 129
Stallion Gate, 101
Stallion Site, 21
Strange Harvest, A, 148
Superman, 162, 165–66
Szasz, Ferenc Morton, 162, 165–67
Szilard, Leo, 154–55

Taos, NM, xiii, 52, 95, 148, 150
Taylor, Mt., 96, 99, 109–10, 143, 169, 178
Teller, Edward, 86, 166, 175
Thelma and Louise, 133
Thermonuclear Monarchy, 87
Thirteen Days, 91
Thompson, Robert Chipper, xiii, xvi
Thoreau, Henry David, 4
Three Mile Island, PA, 58, 111, 115, 120–21
Tolkien, J.R.R., 12
Tourism: eco-, xii, 1, 3, 107; nuclear, xii, 1, 3, 12, 26, 64, 91; toxic, 107
transuranic materials, 41
Tres Piedras, NM, 150
trinitite, 12, 14, 20–21, 24–25
Trinity: A Graphic History of the First

Atomic Bomb, 165
Trinity Site, NM, v-vi, xi, 1, 4, 6–27, 29, 38–40, 84, 96, 101–3, 110, 113, 154, 157, 175–76, 180–82, 184, 189
Truth or Consequences, NM, 37–38
Tsankawi Trail, 74–76
Tucumcari, NM, 88
Tularosa Basin, 9, 103, 183

Udall, Tom, 4, 43, 131
UFO, 54, 107, 152–54, 156
UFO Museum. *See* Roswell UFO Museum
UMTRA. *See* Mexican Hat Uranium Mill Tailings Remedial Site
UNC. *See* United Nuclear Corporation
Underworld, 6, 42
United Nuclear Corporation, 117–19
Up, Up, and Oy Vey! How Jewish History, Culture, and Values Shaped the Comic Book Superheroes, 166
uranium, xi, 3, 90, 96, 103–4, 109–12, 119–21, 124, 130–31, 133–35, 137, 163, 168, 177, 181, 183
USS *Ohio*, 87
Ute, 124

Valdez, Gabe, 146
Valdez, Greg, 144, 146, 148
Valles Caldera, 1, 65, 100
Valley of the Fires, 156–60
vanadium, 130–31, 134–35
Vanadium Corporation of America, 131
Von Braun, Werner, 152

Wagman, Alan, 15, 19
War of the Worlds, 153
Waste Isolation Pilot Plant, 1, 39–44, 46, 48–49, 84, 88, 101, 103
Wasteland, The, 12
Watchmen, v, 167
Wayne, John, 129, 134, 136
Welles, Orson, 153
Wells, H.G., 153–54

White Sands Missile Range, 7, 12, 38
White Sands Missile Range Museum, 38
White Sands National Monument, 38
Wild, Wild West, The, 133
Williams, Terry Tempest, 183
WIPP. *See* Waste Isolation Pilot Plant
witches, 146, 176, 180, 186, 189
World Set Free, The, 155
Woven Stone, 110, 169–70, 184
X-Files, The, 153
X-Men, 167–68

Yeetso, 130
Yucca Mountain, NV, 41–42

Zuni, 176